LOW COUNTRY: BREXIT ON THE ESSEX COAST

Tom Bolton is a writer and researcher. His books and essays include *Vanished City: London's Lost Neighbourhoods, London's Lost Rivers: A Walker's Guide* and *Camden Town: Dreams of Another London.* He has completed a PhD called *Wrong Side of the Tracks? The Development of London's Railway Neighbourhoods.*

PHOTOGRAPHY by Tom Bolton
MAP ILLUSTRATIONS by Oliver Barrett

Low Country

Brexit on the Essex Coast

Tom Bolton

Penned in the Margins

LONDON

PUBLISHED BY PENNED IN THE MARGINS
Toynbee Studios, 28 Commercial Street, London E1 6AB
www.pennedinthemargins.co.uk

First published 2018

Printed in the United Kingdom by TJ International

ISBN
978-1-908058-59-1

THANKS

This is for Jo, who did just as much walking as me.

Many thanks to Tom Chivers at Penned in the Margins for his enthusiasm, expert editing and hard work in making this book what it is.

Thank you to Jeff Barrett and Diva Harris at *Caught by the River*, for publishing the original essays that formed the basis for *Low Country*, and encouraging me to keep writing them.

Thank you to Brian and Toni Dawson, for patiently shepherding us along the Broomway, passing on essential information and bringing us back safely.

Thank you to Peter and Rosalind Bolton for background research, timely ideas and increasingly obscure references.

— TB

CONTENTS

Low Country

Brexit on the Essex Coast

'There are places, just as there are people and objects and works of art, whose relationship of parts creates a mystery.'

PAUL NASH, *OUTLINE* (1949)

INTRODUCTION

On a Friday night in early Spring 2016, Jo and I met after work at Liverpool Street Station to take the train to the Essex coast. We had been walking the coast off and on for several years, using spare weekends and bank holidays to inch our way around the margins of Britain. We were living in south London, where Jo grew up, and to where I had moved after university. Both of us loved the city and lived our lives within its ebb and flow, but we were also drawn away from the centre to the edge, and to the sea. The smooth hills and chalky edges of Sussex and the cliffs, bays and marshes of Kent pulled us from London. So we developed a deceptively simple plan. We would walk along the entire coast of south-east England, through the car parks, sewage works, industrial estates and oil refineries, as well as places designed for day trips. We began by walking out of London along the south bank of the Thames towards the protrusions of Kent, the Sussex havens and cliffs.

I was brought up in a village in the south Warwickshire countryside, in a triangle between Stratford-upon-Avon, Warwick and Leamington Spa. Warwickshire lies deep in the heart of England, as far from the coast as it was possible to retreat, weighted by history and cushioned by geological layers on all sides, rimmed with bands of igneous rock. As a child, I felt the pull from sharper edges at the horizon: the retreating, layered hills to the west, where the Malverns climb towards the Marches, the Black Mountains and, eventually, the distant Welsh coast at Aberdovey and Fishguard, where the Irish Sea bends into the sunset.

We made steady progress. By the end of 2015 Jo and I had walked the coastlines of Kent, East Sussex, West Sussex and Hampshire all the way to the Solent, with a detour to loop around the Isle of Wight. But we had yet to visit Essex. Although close to London, the Essex coastline seems designed to deter the casual visitor. It is little visited and unfashionable, its landscape barely known. Visitors look past Essex to the Areas of Outstanding Natural Beauty in nearby Suffolk, far enough away from London to seem like a proper holiday. The Essex coastline also presents a particular set of physical barriers; multiple broad estuaries, lethal mudflats, coastal reclamation projects, collapsing sea-walls, eroding cliffs, munitions depots, Ministry of Defence firing ranges and seasonal ferries stand in the way of the day tripper. One of the county's largest islands, Foulness, although equipped with a network of public footpaths, can only be reached via a low tide path called The Broomway, a track branded 'the most dangerous footpath in Britain'.

It is often claimed that Essex has the longest coastline of any English county at 350 miles. There is far more of Essex than seems possible. Its estuarine complexity, compounded by the shifting relationship between land and sea, means that the length of its coast changes with the tide and is more or less impossible to measure. Indeed, the very concept of a coastline is inherently unstable; there is no single accepted definition of its physical form. In parts of Essex the high and low tidelines are more than a mile apart.

On a map of northern Europe, Essex is a mirror image of the Netherlands. Each landmass, facing each other across the North Sea, is licked by long tongues of water – low countries of marshland, islands and tidal creeks. This is more than just appearance: the Dutch brought their drainage skills to England in the 16th century, turning Essex into a reclaimed outpost of their own country with a new, firmer coastline protected by long sea-walls.

Essex also specialises in islands. I was intrigued to discover that there are 19 inhabited islands in Essex, from the larger and better known such as Canvey and Mersea, to a host of smaller, inaccessible islands: the off-limits military zone of Foulness and the Essex Archipelago; the privately-owned Osea Island in the Blackwater; semi-accessible nature reserves such as Ray Island,

Skipper's Island and Northey; and a succession of uninhabited or abandoned locations, from Bridgemarsh Island, where the sea came flooding in over the marsh in the 1930s, to Wallasea, where the sea-wall was deliberately breached and much of the island handed back to the sea. And there are also ghost islands, abandoned after catastrophic breaches of their sea-walls, leaving just a trace of their outline on the map.

We could no longer resist the mysteries of a county so near to home. The task would require research and planning. We strung together the trains, buses and, occasionally, taxis that would connect us to the low country of Essex, and calculated routes between overnight stays. We consulted the small canon of Essex coast writing of which a highlight was *350 Miles*, a limited-edition pamphlet of essays by Ken Worpole and desolate photographs by Jason Orton – just the kind of niche literature that leads me to visit obscure places. We identified sites of dereliction to seek out, hidden stories to follow.

During the course of 2016 and 2017, Jo and I walked the 350 miles of the Essex coast – all except those stretches closed to the public by the Army or an encroaching North Sea. We became regular Friday night visitors to Liverpool Street Station, where we boarded trains to Burnham-on-Crouch, Colchester, Thorpe-le-Soken, Walton-on-the-Naze, Harwich and Manningtree. Our starting point was the Essex county boundary at Rainham Marshes, tucked between a landfill site and the M25 motorway crossing. We pushed out along the Thames Estuary past the Crowstone at Southend, an obelisk out on the sands which, half-submerged at high tide, marks the end of the river and the start of the North Sea. As we tracked upstream along estuaries and then downstream along the opposite banks, we became increasingly aware that we had chosen an exceptionally strange time for our walks. Political events – a referendum, surprise elections in Britain and the US and the stream of chaotic blowback that followed – formed the background to our coastal trips. A rising tide of populism took the political establishment completely by surprise. Not only that, but as I walked, I began to realise that these strange events might have unexpected origins in Essex.

Essex is a place everyone thinks they know. It has some of the most familiar stereotypes anywhere in the country, but it seems to date back only a generation. In 1979 Margaret Thatcher entered government thanks to a working-class shift to the Conservatives. It was centred on Essex, and the bellwether constituency of Basildon. On the suburban fringes of London, Basildon and the unglamorous, suburban towns of the London/ Essex fringe were unfashionable and overlooked before 'Essex man', the council-house-buying archetype of the new Tory voter, scorched a new, brash vision of Essex into the culture. Essex found itself both the beneficiary of the new economic boom – Jags and yachts, property investment and sambucas, Florida holidays and Ray-Bans – and the butt of the joke. Essex man and Essex girl knew what they enjoyed, could afford to buy it, and did not care what anyone else thought. They were easily mocked, most notably by sketch comedian Harry Enfield, whose character 'Loadsamoney' instantly became part of the 1980s' highlights reel. Thirty years on, the reality TV series *The Only Way is Essex*, so popular it is only known by its initials, has recycled the same themes as parody. One of its stars, Joey Essex, is named after the place he comes from and is famous for being stupid.

The Essex story has consumed itself, but the politics burns more fiercely than ever. I knew that beyond the reductive media images, Essex has a quite different history: of radical politics, social experiment and alternative ways of living. It has been a place of exile, where progressive thinkers and artists have retreated to shape their philosophies. The path was from city to country, Londoners moving east to see things differently. Working-class east London had moved, often without much choice, into the Essex suburbs after the Second World War. However, this new, forward-looking society built on socialism, new towns and new ways of living had also seeded Thatcher's counter-revolution. Then, in the early 1990s, a group of Essex MPs ignited the anti-European movement with their opposition to the Maastricht Treaty agreement negotiated by John Major's Conservative government, to which they belonged. Major's time may seem distant now but the Maastricht rebels have never really gone away; their ideas spawned UKIP, the EU referendum of 2016 and the march towards Brexit. People underestimated by the country as a whole, and the capital in particular, have taken a grip on national politics and identity in a way that seems certain to define an era. Essex is more than political caricature and London overspill. The east of the county is remote, and the long stretches between seaside resorts little visited by outsiders. The opening lines of J.A. Baker's Essex nature book *The Peregrine* describe the dividing line between country and marshland Essex: 'East of my home, the long ridge lies across the skyline like the low hull of a submarine. Above it, the eastern sky is bright with reflections of distant water, and there is a feeling of sails beyond land.' Hidden downwind of London, in the shadow of its suburbs, the coastal areas remain obscure.

During our entire time on the Essex coast we did not encounter anyone else who seemed to be engaged in long-distance walking. Local walkers emerged close to settlements, often with dogs, soon dropping away as we passed out again into the marshes. Farmers crossed our path, almost always in the far distance. I later discovered that Worpole had predicted our project, astutely identifying those 'who have returned to exploring the terrain on foot ... a new kind of secular pilgrimage, based on immersion.' Our walk was exactly that. It provided space for thinking and the consolation of the outdoors, which proved welcome as our sense of reality and our understanding of the country we lived in was undermined by the referendum, the election of Donald Trump in the US and the polarisation of politics into Remainers and Leavers, Liberals and the Alt-Right, us and them. In Essex, big skies and distant horizons seemed to offer release and, perhaps, the freedom to see our country more clearly.

I

GATEWAY

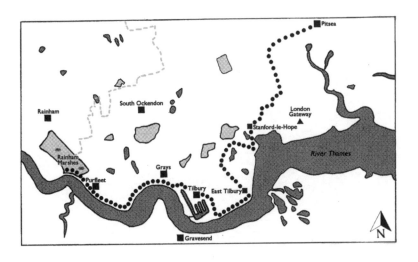

THE LINE OF THE ESSEX COUNTY BOUNDARY across Rainham Marshes Nature Reserve is marked only by a collapsed chainlink fence, an abandoned border crossing. Its crooked cement posts fixed both the end of London and the start of our journey along the Essex coast. As Jo and I crossed the boundary fence and walked to the edge of the reserve, a sleeping bag lay discarded in the middle of the path and, further along, a fire site blackened the earth. High above us, an early skylark twittered and purred like a busy modem. We paused, looking towards Dagenham. The Thames was dwindling into the distance. Then we turned east to begin our 350-mile walk to the other end of Essex, following its meandering coast all the way. Our first walk would take us to Benfleet, halfway up the Thames in the direction of Southend-on-Sea. As we crossed the boundary, Jo felt a strange, electric tingling along her arm. There was a charge in the air.

We had set ourselves a project, to walk the Essex coast, attracted by the lure of the overlooked, of places that no one bothered to visit. I was also intrigued by the idea of marshes, an unfamiliar setting with undertones of mystery and danger. To begin our journey, Jo and I headed for Purfleet, on the Thames Estuary. The boundary between the London Borough of Havering and the County of Essex lies halfway across the leftover slice of wetland at

Rainham, deep among the estuary's industrial landscapes. Most people pass through on their way to Southend, but the estuary has its own, dedicated railway line, the C2C, that leads nowhere else; it threads east among riverside logistics parks, power stations and overpasses, passing through east London on a viaduct beside the Thames to Southend and Shoeburyness, where both the river and the line come to an end. Beyond lies only white space on the map, merging into the light brown of mudflats, where sea and land become hard to separate. The spread of the light brown is as large as the white, pushing out across the North Sea channels.

Many of the capital's noxious industries are to be found alongside the estuary in the outer boroughs of Barking and Dagenham and Havering, as well as under the shadow of the M25 bridge. They lie in the Thames Gateway, an area optimistically rebranded in the late 1990s to welcome housing estates and new town centres that have proved slow to arrive. Since the industrial revolution Essex has been a convenient place to dump anything London does not need or want: from toxic waste shipped to landfill to effluent pumped into the Thames by machines such as those found at the ornate, Victorian pumping station at Crossness.

Essex is also very flat. John Norden, writing in 1594, observed that '[i]n this shire are no great store of hills.' The railway journey gave us a high-line tour from the viaduct, revealing abandoned works huts, invisible from the street, and offering close-up views of rumpled sheets in chain hotel bedrooms. We passed through Dagenham Dock into territories unknown. This is where industrial London has ended up, squeezed out of the centre to the very edges. There were almost no people to be seen, only Eddie Stobart lorries and Canute tankers parked up beside impossibly large grey and pastel warehouses. The tankers advertised: 'Personal solutions for you, wherever you are in the world.'

On the train, Jo read an article about the variable nature of time. Time, she told me, passes more slowly at sea level than higher up, for example in the mountains. The difference in the distance rotated by the Earth can be measured by placing clocks at contrasting altitudes. The clocks show a small disparity that grows over time. Life passes more quickly at altitude, and a person spending their time in the mountains lives and ages faster. At sea level – zero feet – there is more time, whether or not anyone realises. The literal pace of life differs from place to place, and slowest of all was the route we would be taking, as close to sea level as the path would take us.

We left the train at Purfleet, the first town in Essex, in long-term transition from a military base and port to something else, still to be defined. Creative industries were welcomed to

Thurrock, now the town's preferred name. The Royal Opera House in London had moved its scenery workshops here some years before, but the anticipated cultural economy remains elusive. Meanwhile, in 2014 the World Health Organisation reported that this area had the highest levels of particulate air pollution in the UK.

Purfleet is synonymous with the Esso Fuel Terminal. Its hulking storage tanks dominate the riverfront, surrounded by tracks of cleared land. Railway Cottages, the 19th-century terraces

opposite the station, had been boarded up and marked as 'acquired for development', with the exception of one lone, cussed house in the middle, still occupied.

This was our first visit to Rainham Marshes. Separated from Purfleet by the culverted Mardyke, the marshes are said to resemble the pre-industrial state of the Thames basin. Before drainage, development and embankment, the river was wider and slower than it is now and washed across much of inner south

London at high tide. The pre-urban landscape was good for duck hunting but poor for staying dry. London's marshes were drained and pushed to the very edge of the city, leaving Rainham as a remnant connecting Greater London to Essex.

We crossed a wooden bridge to an elevated hide operated by the Royal Society for the Protection of Birds (RSPB), an observation platform with a wetland vista, backed by power stations, overpasses, pylons and sluice gates. Visitors were recording the migrating birds that come and go from Africa and Europe, stopping at Rainham on their bi-annual global trips. A whiteboard reported the day's spots in black marker, with coloured bird illustrations. Willow, sedge and reed warblers were arriving on the marshes. Terns were fishing on the river. With a pair of huge binoculars, a volunteer showed me a solitary Great Egret in the far distance that looked like a scrubbed heron.

It was immediately clear to us that Rainham had been a Ministry of Defence firing range, disused and reclaimed for public use. An array of rifle targets still stood on the marsh topped with carved, greying numbers. In 1990, Rainham had been seriously considered as a location for a theme park run by the American company Universal Studios. Twenty-five years on, Paramount Pictures is planning a park on the opposite bank, in Dartford. Regular gunfire echoed over the site from the Kent bank, where the remaining shooting range on Dartford Marshes was busy. The embanked path ran along a sea-wall and was dotted with small groups of birders, mostly men in safari jackets and floppy sunhats, carrying telescopes in their own miniature rain covers. Jo and I took the path across the reserve, beside the Thames, towards the rounded, green hill of the former landfill site, studded with black plastic vents. A group of young men headed around the perimeter fence towards the Ford plant at Dagenham, each carrying a can of cider and a cigarette.

In the river beside the reserve, we spotted a series of tar black posts standing in grey mud, the remains of a 6,000-year-old forest. A tangle of tree trunks – ash, elm and alder – are preserved in brown peat beneath the river mud. The trees belong to the Neolithic era, and flint tools found here hint at hunter-gatherers who roamed the Thames shore. The relict forest links this coastline straight back to a darker, wilder place far beyond the edge of recorded history. The ancient stumps – astonishing archaeology, noticed by almost no one – seemed to me a sign that this was a good place to be searching for the underside of Britain.

We left Rainham Marshes, passing the single surviving building of the Royal Gunpowder Magazines complex. Purfleet had been the central storage facility for Britain's gunpowder from the Napoleonic Wars to the Second World War. It was housed in five magazine warehouses, specially constructed to resist bombardment, each containing more than 10,000 barrels of powder. The information board noted that workers had not been allowed to smoke. Purfleet Barracks, once nearby, had vanished without trace, but the riverside housing that had replaced them faithfully replicated the Barracks' atmosphere.

I knew Purfleet through *Dracula*, which was surely its trump card. Bram Stoker located Carfax House, the count's estuary residence, in Purfleet and it was here that he had come

ashore in boxes of earth shipped from Transylvania. It is likely that Stoker had actually visited Purfleet, a popular Victorian day trip destination from London, and appropriated its dark, secluded atmosphere. 'It is surrounded by a high wall, of ancient structure, built of heavy stones, and has not been repaired for a large number of years. The closed gates are of heavy old oak and iron, all eaten with rust.' However, Stoker had fictionalised the setting so that no ideal model for Carfax House could be found, and there was certainly no associated Goth festival as in Whitby. The painter

Jock McFadyen's 2001 work *From Dracula's Garden* presents a view of the Thames Estuary dominated by the distant, smoking form of the castle-like Coryton Refinery, visible to the east on the Essex skyline. Purfleet had put up a blue plaque nonetheless, beside the main road, and the Dracula connection drifted in the diesel from cars ploughing through the small centre, as we tracked away from Rainham Marshes.

The Queen Elizabeth Bridge carries the M25 motorway over the Thames, passing high over Thurrock and crashing to earth far in the distance, an epic urban structure like the New Jersey Turnpike or the Brooklyn Bridge but without an accompanying city. Beneath its concrete span, West Thurrock is one long service centre, where the logos of two key players in the politics and economy of 21st-century Britain, Amazon and the Daily Mail, are emblazoned on a succession of otherwise indistinguishable, corrugated grey units of astonishing size. As we trekked along the estuary, the traffic on the bridge streamed over the river and entire neighbourhoods in a single sweep. The fuel that powers the cars and lorries is stored in the huddle of white steel cylinders that make up the Grays Oil Storage Depot. Beyond, the small town of Grays is dominated by the vast, disused State Cinema, an art deco complex built in 1938.

Life has been sucked from Grays, vampire-style, by the neighbouring retail black hole at Lakeside, Thurrock. The State Cinema has been saved from a generation of decay by Wetherspoon's, which is converting the building into an enormous pub. Tim Martin, the chain's owner, had recently stepped up his anti-EU rhetoric and was planning an active role in the referendum campaign to come. Later, he was to accuse 'an elite, mostly graduates of Oxford or Cambridge Universities' of 'groupthink' and indulgence in a 'quasi-religion' in their support of the EU. His comments, combining a grain of truth with a vast helping of parody, distilled the mood of the moment to perfection.

Grays is tucked into the inside of a bend in the Thames. Where it turns back east we cut inland to walk around the perimeter of Tilbury Docks. Tilbury is Britain's Ellis Island, the port where the repurposed troopship Empire Windrush docked from Jamaica in 1948, carrying not only passengers from the West Indies, but a group of 66 Poles. They had travelled all the way around the world to escape Nazi Germany, arriving in Britain via Siberia, the Pacific and Mexico before joining the Windrush in Jamaica. American poet Denise Levertov described the emigration that had drawn her family through Essex on their way across the Atlantic: 'Something forgotten twenty years: although my fathers / and mothers came from Cordova and Vitesk and Caernarvon,

/ and although I am a citizen of the United States and less a / stranger here than anywhere else, perhaps / I am Essex born.' Tilbury had none of the tourist buzz of Ellis Island. Instead, it was just the two of us, marching around the fence that kept us away from the container stacks, and three boys in a hurry, one of whom, for reasons best known to himself, was carrying a crowbar.

At Tilbury, we spotted an even larger Amazon warehouse squatting beside the railway line. Tilbury Power Station is separated from the Thames by a concrete sea barrier. The path between wall and river, around the power station's hard security line. It was painted from end-to-end with murals only visible to those who passed close by, the scale all the more surprising for being hidden away. Pleasantly surprised by the outbreak of wild colours in a landscape of grey concrete and mud, we photographed Asterix and Obelix, Homer Simpson and a selection of Mod revival symbols and slogans. A full-size version of Roy Lichtenstein's pop art painting *Whaam!* was fading away like the residue of the explosion it portrayed. Beyond was the wide estuary, and the distant Kentish shore.

Before the better-remembered periods in his life as a writer, dissenter and spy, Daniel Defoe ran a brickworks at Tilbury. He lived in a farmhouse on the marshes nearby and described his neighbourhood in the 1720s in *A Tour Through the Whole Island of*

Great Britain. Between Barking and Dagenham, he recorded, 'The famous breach, made by an inundation of the Thames, which was so great, as that it laid near 5,000 acres of land under water.' The floodwaters remained for 10 years until the breach was eventually repaired by one Captain Perry, fresh from engineering for the Czar of Russia on the River Don. Even this close to London, the Essex coastline is vulnerable, dependent on hard engineering to keep it intact.

Leaving the docks, we encountered Tilbury Fort, incongruously squeezed between a distribution park with a wind turbine and sewage works. The fort was built for Charles II and later described by Defoe as 'a water bastion ... the largest of England.' It was London's main defence from Thames invaders until the Second World War. An impressive double moat and fortifications cut decorative star shapes into the marsh. Before the fort was constructed, this site was where Elizabeth I had famously addressed troops preparing for a Spanish invasion, making her 'body of a weak and feeble woman; heart and stomach of a king' speech. There are few sites in Britain with such an engrained place in island history – Hastings, Runnymede maybe, Sir Francis Drake's bowling lawn – but to us it existed as a notional location, detached from geography and floating somewhere among a world of history book illustrations for children. At the perimeter of the fort, a white, weatherboarded pub sat beside the river in strange isolation: The World's End.

After the sewage works, the flat lands lay before us and, for the first time, we experienced the strange sensation of walking along a sea-wall, balanced on an endless ridge. This would later become very familiar. The path was positioned above the surrounding countryside on an earth embankment, sometimes topped with a concrete path. This would revert without warning to tall, thick grass, a struggle to pass through. We could see its course

running away far ahead of us. Rather than becoming absorbed into the landscape through walking, the sea-wall separated us and kept us constantly aware of our elevated position.

Donkeys grazed on East Tilbury marshes, under the super-sized pylons that crowded towards the generator hall. At the power station, the parked trucks were marked in bold lettering: Prestons of Potto, Bartrums, Wincanton. The power station had been converted from coal in 2012, to burn biomass and wood pellets instead. A stack of these had ignited a major fire in 2013, and the

power station had been mothballed. Its twin chimneys, with the single stack at Littlebrook on the opposite bank, were the tallest structures in Essex. I was disappointed when, 18 months after our visit, they were demolished in controlled explosions, watched from Kent by crowds on the Gravesend promenade. Replacement gas turbines were planned for the site. The Littlebrook chimney, the last of a succession of elegant sentinel chimneys which had dominated the flat estuary, was also scheduled for demolition.

On East Tilbury Marshes, we passed the Coalhouse Fort, a round stone battery, open in the centre, with a half-moat as an extra barrier to attacks from the river. It was one of 'Palmerston's Follies', forts built in the 1860s on the orders of the Prime Minister, Lord Palmerston, to defend against French invasion under Napoleon III, which never came. The Coalhouse Fort had eventually come into use during the Second World War as an anti-aircraft gun site, and was equipped with heavy guns taken from HMS Hood, the Navy's last heavy cruiser. A line of mines had been laid across the Thames from the fort to the Kent shore.

The year before, I had come across an exhibition programme called 'Radical Essex', run by the Focal Point Gallery in Southend, which aimed to illuminate the county's forgotten history as the home of Modernist experiments in architecture and living. The disused Bata Factory outside Tilbury was a poignant reminder of this aspect of the county's history. We made a detour off the line of the coast to see East Tilbury, a company town built by the Czech Bata shoe company in 1932. The company was once the world's largest shoe maker and its founder, Tomáš Baťa, established factories around the world, from India to Canada, accompanied by garden town-style developments for workers. The East Tilbury factory closed in 2005. The town is built around the slab-like main block, its mournful streets with their boxy houses spreading out in a grid pattern.

We walked along the high street past the factory, which also contained the town's small selection of shops on its ground floor. It looked to me like the set for a documentary on post-industrial dystopia. East Tilbury claims to be the first Modernist development in Britain, a pioneering new town inspired by the machine efficiency which was the Bata company's rationale. Unfortunately, without the factory the town had lost its raison d'être and instead acquired an atmosphere of behind-the-Iron-Curtain decay. A little further along the river, we passed the grassy hills of Mucking Marshes. The hills had a strange appearance, the new vegetation and unnatural smoothness clearly concealing something. Mucking was once the largest landfill site in western Europe. Closed and capped in 2010, thick grass now grew over more than a century of London's refuse, brought there on barges from Walbrook Wharf, in the City of London, their contents unrecorded until the 1990s. No one knows quite what is buried there.

Now we detoured inland, following the same footpath which had, until this point, tracked the river. We were tiring, feeling the miles in our legs, so we stopped in Stanford-le-Hope. The newly married Joseph Conrad and his wife, Jessie, had set up house there in 1896, shortly after Conrad had left the merchant navy to become a full-time writer. They stayed for only two years, but Conrad began work on *Heart of Darkness* in Stanford. Its opening, on board the Nellie moored in the Thames Estuary, is set in the landscape he knew: 'The water shone pacifically; the sky, without a speck, was a benign immensity of unstained light; the very mist on the Essex marsh was like a gauzy and radiant fabric, hung from the wooded rises inland, and draping the low shores in diaphanous folds. Only the gloom to the west, brooding over the upper reaches, became more sombre every minute, as if angered by the approach of the sun.' The Thames connects London to its imperial possessions and, in *Heart of Darkness*, Conrad linked it directly to the shadow it cast over the far edges of the known world.

We found Stanford disconcerting. It was picture postcard-pretty, with a handsome church, weather-boarded houses and a war memorial. When we entered a pub, the atmosphere was wired and oddly threatening, the clientele mostly men who were drinking fast for a Sunday lunchtime, standing up. Someone threw a comment in our direction, of which we only caught the gist, but it did not seem friendly. Wearing walking gear and carrying rucksacks we felt conspicuous and slightly absurd, having wandered unthinkingly into a place that did not belong to us. We made our stop a quick one and pressed on out of Stanhope, forced away from the estuary around Vange Marshes, Bowers Marshes and Vange Creek, an area of sudden flatness described, perhaps harshly, by Daniel Defoe as 'justly said to be both unhealthy, and unpleasant.'

The detour took us around the site of London's new megaport, London Gateway; we could see its cranes on the horizon. The 'fully integrated logistics facility' was built by Dubai-based DP World to handle new, extra-large container ships. London's river trade has been increasing in size and retreating further from the city for many decades and this is the new port of London, superseding Tilbury Docks. Construction began in 2010 and was still in progress as we passed. It involved realigning the shore, using sand dredged from beneath the sea to extend it out into the Thames. The land itself is malleable, created where there was none before and this, as we would discover, is the model for the entire Essex coast. The land is a constant state of erosion and loss, reclamation and reuse, confounding expectations that a landscape should provide solidity from era to era.

We skirted the small village of Fobbing, where the Peasants' Revolt had begun in 1381 when villagers, led by Thomas Baker, refused to pay the Poll Tax demanded by a visiting tax collector. The uprising that followed involved bands from Essex and from Kent, the latter led by the notorious Wat Tyler. The revolt ended with defeat and the execution of Tyler at Smithfield in London, but Baker was also hanged and drawn at Chelmsford for his involvement, so we thought it unfair that Wat Tyler Country Park at the head of the creek was named after the Kentish man instead. Reaching Pitsea Station, we sank gratefully into the C2C's embrace. The first leg of our Essex journey had taken us through a strange and sometimes hostile territory. This was London's 'hidden reverse', the place where the mechanisms behind the illusions were tucked safely away. Laid out on the basis that no one would think to come there, the Thames Estuary was both a non-place and somewhere with a powerful, unexpected presence. We had mixed feelings but had never been anywhere like it, and we had barely begun our journey.

II

ESTUARY

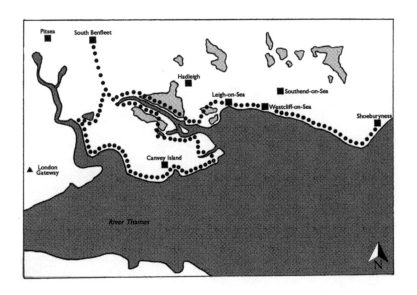

A COUPLE OF WEEKS LATER we returned to Benfleet, the station for Canvey Island. We had visited Canvey before, when a walk around its perimeter turned out to be a stranger experience than we had expected – raised on the sea-wall, the estuary and sky equally, impossibly vast, observing the houses of Canvey from above. John, the narrator in Terry Taylor's 1961 novel *Barons Court, All Change*, observed, 'My mum's bungalow was called "Seaview", but you couldn't view the sea because of the sea-wall.' A good 13 miles around, Canvey was entirely surrounded by the wall, which was all that prevented it from becoming water too. The island within was a deep saucer, and we balanced on its rim, raised above the boats, the houses, the caravans, the sea itself.

Despite its precariousness as reclaimed land, it is thought that Canvey has been inhabited since at least Roman times. It is suggested that the Roman astronomer Ptolemy described Canvey in his map of Albion, produced during the 2nd century A.D. The map included the co-ordinates for 'Counus Island', which he described as 'east of the Trinovantes', the Celtic tribe of Essex. This may have been Canvey, which was also associated with the 'Council Island' where the Trinovantes met the Iceni of Norfolk, the Cantiaci of Kent and the Catuvellaini from west Essex and Hertfordshire before Boudicca's rebellion in 60 A.D.

Canvey is an island with a defiant character, drawn from

its struggle with the sea, a conflict that has sometimes turned very bitter indeed. It is no coincidence that the cadaverous patron saint of Canvey is Dr Feelgood bassist Wilko Johnson, who was diagnosed with terminal pancreatic cancer in 2013 but has, miraculously, been cured and is still alive. Canvey is an isolated place, connected by a bridge to the mainland, projecting on its own into the Thames. Before the bridge opened in 1931, it could be reached by ferry at high water or, at low water, by wading through the mud. The island had recently become the subject of media attention when it was revealed that 100 families of ultra-Orthodox Jews from London's Stamford Hill had decided to relocate as a community to Canvey, where property was cheaper and more easily available. There was speculation over how a place associated with traditional ideas of Englishness would deal with the arrival of people whose rationale would be to live separately, next door to Canvey's existing inhabitants.

Terry Taylor reported that 'Canvey Island has a lonely look. Its prom, its main road, its side streets can be swallowed up by people – yet, it still looks lonely. It tries hard to look like a holiday resort, but it fails.' The island was putting on a front, but it was no surprise if it seemed a little hollow. Only a few years before Taylor's novel, Canvey had experienced the defining, catastrophic event in its modern existence.

Thursday 29th January 1953 was the day when a depression labelled Low Z was first recorded in the mid-Atlantic. That night it merged with a second depression, Low G, south of Iceland, and began to move slowly towards Scotland. By the afternoon of Friday 30th January, a south-west wind was pushing the waters of the North Sea towards the still-deepening depression, while at the same time a new wind drove the waters of the Atlantic in from the west. By Saturday morning, Low Z had become a 'trough of depression' and was moving south, now chased by a high-pressure ridge, High A. The gale it brought was the strongest then recorded, reaching hurricane force across the entire British Isles. In Orkney gusts reached 125mph, while in Southampton the strength of the wind prevented the Queen Mary from leaving port.

In Essex, things did not seem right on the River Blackwater at Maldon. A police constable reported that the wind was so strong it was holding the water in place, and the afternoon tide appeared not to have gone out. High tide was still coming though, a wall of water driven down the North Sea by the pressure ridge. Alarm began to spread south around 5.30pm as the surge hit the coast, topping sea defences in Northumberland and East Yorkshire. Lincolnshire towns flooded next, and then, as the tide in The Wash rose eight feet higher than usual, defences broke south of King's Lynn and 65 people, mostly American servicemen and their families, drowned as their bungalows were swept out to sea. In Suffolk, the surge pushed the cliffs at Lowestoft back by 40 feet.

As we reached the south-west corner of Canvey and the Thames Estuary, we saw the island at its oddest. The white weatherboarded Lobster Smack was one of the oldest buildings on the island, dating to the late 16th century and said to be the dubious inn that provided refuge to Pip and Magwitch in Charles Dickens'

Great Expectations. Across Holehaven Creek lay the giant tanks, jetties and flares of the Coryton Oil Refinery, Canvey's long-term neighbour. Beyond, the gantry cranes of the London Gateway port, lined up on the horizon, stood larger than anything else in the landscape.

We rounded the south-west corner of the island and walked along Canvey's prime seafront. The Labworth Café stood defiantly above the sea-wall, a piece of lean, elegant Modernism from 1933, the only building designed solo by famed engineer Ove

Arup. With its round, central viewing deck, the café mimicked the bridge of the Queen Mary herself. It now peers anxiously over the concrete sea defences, which were raised in the aftermath of the Great Storm, reducing the café's height by a storey.

Work began on the wall around Canvey in 1623, when Canvey's landowners agreed that the tidal island, divided into two sections by a creek, would be 'inned' or reclaimed from the sea. Hundreds of Dutch engineers, already engaged in draining the Fens of East Anglia, built walls of clay, chalk and Kentish ragstone around the island, and constructed sluices to control the water levels. In payment for their work, many settled on Canvey. Some streets still carry Dutch names, although others were added at the turn of the century in an attempt to attract visitors to 'Little Holland'. An 1893 article described 'the curious impression of having sailed into a small Dutch haven by mistake,' with Dutch eel boats putting in on their way to Billingsgate. The relationship has not always been cosy, however; in 1667, during the Anglo-Dutch War, the Dutch navy attacked the English fleet at anchor on the Medway and sent a party up the Thames to Canvey Island, where they burned houses and barns, and stole sheep.

Our route took us right back to where we started. As we crossed back to the mainland we felt that Canvey was almost trapped by its own crucial sea defences. From lower ground behind the wall, the sea itself was obscured. In Canvey an ambivalent relationship with the sea is understandable. The Great Flood hit worst of all. The storm had reached Harwich, the northernmost point in Essex, at 11pm on the night of 29th January, and it was clear that something out of the ordinary was happening. The tide had not yet peaked, but the harbourmaster reported that it was already so high that it had broken the tide gauge. News from the north had not been passed on quickly enough, and by the time the inhabitants of Walton, Clacton, Jaywick, Brightlingsea, Mersea, Foulness, Canvey, Tilbury and Thurrock heard what was coming their way, it was too late to act. When the BBC finally broadcast an alert on the midnight news, the sea had already flooded the high-water mark along the entire Essex coast, from the northern edge at Manningtree on the Stour to the Royal Docks on the Thames Estuary, where London then began. A second wave of water hit Harwich at 12.20am. By 2am the coastal towns were underwater, and sea defences breached in 839 separate places. The floods killed 307 people on land throughout the country, and a further 224 when the Princess Victoria ferry sank in the Irish Sea. One hundred and nineteen people were drowned in Essex, including 58 on Canvey and 37 at Jaywick. On the opposite side of the North Sea in the Netherlands, 1,835 people died, a disaster of a magnitude not seen since the 1400s. In Britain, Canvey

Island, now entirely underwater, became the iconic image of the Flood.

The Great Flood is still well within living memory, a civic disaster which turned the world's attention to the east of England and to the Essex coast. Hilda Grieve's 850-page account of the floods, published in 1959, is a masterpiece of social history. She records the events of the Great Flood in precise, sequential detail. It is a compelling, horrifying read, and a quintessential Essex book which comes to a reckoning with the sea.

Grieve sets the scene with her first sentence: 'Essex and the sea have been antagonists for centuries.' In matter-of-fact manner, she takes as her starting point a period 3,350 million years in the past, to which 'the formation of the earth's crust' could be dated. Her history of the Essex landscape builds from this point, speeding through the ages to record disastrous floods and recurring attempts to hold back the sea. Then her account slows from a grand sweep to an hour-by-hour, and then a minute-by-minute, account of events on the one day that matters.

East of Benfleet and Canvey, the coast opened out into an unmistakable combination of tidal mudflats, low marshy ground and glittering estuary waters. On a ridge above the marsh, the ruins of Hadleigh Castle appeared like the jagged landmark painted by John Constable after the death of his wife Maria, his grief reflected in the stormy setting. England was once effectively ruled from Hadleigh, which was built by Hubert de Burgh, unofficial regent to the infant king Henry III. Later, it had been a favourite residence of Edward III, and played an important strategic role during the Hundred Years' War; it is one of the earliest in a succession of defensive installations from multiple eras now to be found crumbling along the Essex coast.

The ruins now mark the grounds of Hadleigh Temple, which belonged to the Salvation Army. This was the first of several experimental communes we would encounter during our journey, and the only one still in operation. General Booth, founder of the Salvation Army, turned to new models of living as a way to help the poorest of the poor, 'the submerged tenth'. He set up 'farm colonies' at Hadleigh on the Thames Estuary in 1891 and Boxted, in Dedham Vale, in 1902. Unlike the socialist and anarchist versions we would later discover, these were patrician institutions where those who had fallen into the temptations of the East End were kept well away from alcohol and prostitutes, and were given work to occupy body and mind and to prepare them for the future. At Hadleigh, the clock in the head office window bore the slogan 'Every Hour for Jesus'.

Hadleigh is now used by the Salvation Army to provide training. At its peak, the colony was home to 500 people who worked 3,000 acres of farmland and operated a brickworks. Its purpose was not to reshape society in Britain but to export people overseas, where they could start again – an aim also pursued by union activists on the Dengie. Hadleigh was intended to prepare the destitute for a new life in the colonies and was laid out like a military compound, with officers' quarters, a hospital, dormitories, mess hall, library and lecture hall arranged around a central citadel. Sir Henry Rider Haggard, the 19th-century adventure novelist, also carried out extensive studies as a prospective agricultural reformer, attempting to diagnose the country's social and economic ills. He visited Hadleigh and was impressed, particularly approving of the colony's aspirational class system, designed to incentivise good behaviour through the lure of promotion from lower to upper.

Hidden almost too low in the landscape for us to see, Two Tree Island lies between Hadleigh Marsh and Leigh Sand. It is another former landfill site, which closed in the 1970s. The island is now a nature reserve, but the toxic waste dumped there means that access had been restricted for years. The island's eponymous two trees were elms, blown down in a storm during the 1960s. Elms had once been prominent across the Essex marshlands, but have almost entirely disappeared as a result of the arrival of Dutch Elm Disease in the late 1960s. Fruit trees can now be found across the island instead – apple, plum and pear trees seeded from London's rubbish bins.

We entered the final stretch of the Thames Estuary with the Southend seafront, which begins at Leigh-on-Sea and stretches, unbroken, for 6 miles to Shoeburyness. This was our

destination, where the mysterious Essex marshes truly began. Leigh felt disconcertingly urban after the disjointed edgelands that had taken us all the way from Purfleet and Rainham Marshes. We walked into riverside Leigh: cobbled street, boats, oysters and a pub called Ye Olde Smack. The riverside is a 'ye olde' village, a tiny blob on the map surrounded by the rest of Leigh, a town many times its size, an octopus of avenues filled with inter-war semis. With no separation that we could discern, Leigh became Westcliff-on-Sea, then Chalkwell, Southend-on-Sea, Southchurch, Thorpe

Bay, Shoebury and Shoeburyness without a pause.

The Thames is still officially river and not sea until it reaches an invisible line in the estuary, connecting Westcliff and the Isle of Grain in Kent. The boundary is also where the jurisdiction of the Port of London Authority ends and is marked with a stone on either side. On the Kent coast a small obelisk sits in the middle of nowhere, in the mud of Yantlet Creek, and is known as the London Stone. We passed the Essex version, the Crowstone, in a rather more accessible spot on the beach at Westcliff, handy for the promenade. The Crowstone Crawl is a popular route for Southend swimmers, but the stone itself, which pokes above the water even at high tide, is a replacement from the 1950s, its predecessor long retired to nearby Priory Park.

We made our way to the far end of Southend Pier, the longest pleasure pier in the world, reaching 1.3 miles out into the Thames. It is long enough to have its own train service, but its main function for us was to emphasise the width of the river mouth. At the end of the pier the Kentish shore – the Isle of Grain – felt no closer than it did from the promenade. At the foot of the pier Adventure Island is the full English of seaside fairgrounds, with surreal entertainment on an unlikely scale. Crazy golf involves playing around a full-sized helicopter and a crashed Cessna. The arcades on the promenade are enormous, with names such as New York, Monte Carlo, Electric Avenue and Happidrome. Pubs are frequent, small and, as we passed, packed, with families standing outside, drinking together. A little further along, the Kursaal appeared like a relic from an earlier age, a domed building from 1901 which had been one of the world's earliest and largest amusement parks. Its German name dated it firmly to the pre-First World War era, when the German cultural presence in Britain had been stronger than it was now possible to imagine.

The seafront had all the classic elements of the English seaside resort but, despite its holiday atmosphere, it was also part of industrial Essex, upstream and downwind. It was in the open-air swimming pool at Southend that a young Ian Dury, later lead singer of the Blockheads, contracted polio while on a day trip from Upminster. In her poem 'Essex Kiss', Lavinia Greenlaw encapsulated the coastal industrial atmospherics of Southend: 'Chewing gum and whelks, a whiff / of diesel, crocus, cuckoo spit.'

Greenlaw knows these Essex resorts with their arcades and cheap thrills, and knows the darkness that emerged when their lights failed; she grew up south of Chelmsford in the 1970s. She recalled the absolute blackness of power cuts, as well as the grey of hours spent waiting for buses or looking for a lift. 'I think of

Essex as a place you can't get out of easily.' Southend is out on a limb, with nowhere to go either south or east, and it feels like a place where the only choices are to remain or to return the way you came.

Further out to sea, somewhere beyond Shoeburyness, is where aerial photographs show the muddy waters of the Thames dispersing, their colour changing from brown to blue as the river meets the North Sea. Jonathan Raban, sailing around the coast of Britain in the late 1980s, reported that a line of rubbish floats just below the surface, marking the line where the tidal flow of the river peters out. He claimed to have seen a car seat there, 'placidly swivelling on its own.' East Anglian painter Michael Andrews's *Thames Estuary*, produced in 1995 as he was dying from cancer, is part map, part hallucination; the shore is muddy teal, and men in boats of an indistinguishable era fish at the edge of reality beside a sea whose surface glows from a light shining from somewhere in the far distance, outside the frame. One of the figures stands alone in his boat, which appears to be a ferry.

As we passed into Shoeburyness, the spread of Southend ended abruptly, and the last tip of land before the coast turned north was wide open and empty, apart from the 19th-century military buildings that came into view. This was the original site of the Shoebury Garrison, commanding the mouth of the Thames

Estuary. When the Crimean War broke out in 1851, the Royal Artillery School of Gunnery had been established, and a barracks, officers' quarters, hospital and church built. Foulness has now been taken over by QinetiQ, a defence contractor that now operates the firing range for the Ministry of Defence. The site is no longer managed by the Shoeburyness Garrison. It felt strangely unresolved, with a suburban road crossing low grassland to an area of new housing and the original Royal Artillery buildings, on a scale of grandeur unmatched by anything we had encountered on our walk so far. The old army presence – parade-ground lawns, Victorian villas, buildings identified by letters and memorials – was powerful. The very edge of Essex is still military territory, although Countryside and Metropolitan house-builders had pushed a brand-new estate into one of its corners.

The original gunnery site closed in 1976, and the firing ranges are now located on the empty marshlands of the Essex Archipelago, the mysterious, semi-accessible tidal islands to the north. Foulness, the largest of all the islands, is entirely off-limits to the public, except for those willing to brave the exceptionally dangerous tidal footpath, The Broomway. We considered navigating the footpath by ourselves, but it was no longer marked out with sprigs of broom and it did not take long for us to realise we would be entirely out of our comfort zones. The nature writer

Robert Macfarlane has walked this route without a guide and survived the experience. But we lacked the controlled recklessness of the true explorer, and felt only that we were letting ourselves down.

Unlike the much better-known tidal footpath across Morecambe Bay, there were no official guides to the Broomway. Far from being a tourist attraction, the public are strongly discouraged from attempting the route. The changing tides, dependent on lunar calendar and weather conditions, shifting, soft mud, and abandoned munitions make the path spectacularly hazardous; many people are recorded to have drowned on their way to Foulness. In the 1920s, before the MoD bridge was built, the Broomway was the only way to reach the island without a boat. The postman, with his pony and trap, had followed the tide out to be sure he had time to return to the mainland.

We looped back to Shoeburyness and boarded a C2C. The train slid all the way back along the estuary towards London, tracking the route we had walked. It felt essential to the logic of our project that we find a way into this most remote of locations, but we wanted to survive the experience. Not long after we returned home, I discovered an Essex couple who led occasional guided walks along the Broomway in their spare time. They were the only people who guided on the route anymore, and were close to retirement. We decided we must visit the Essex Archipelago with them later that summer, rather than braving it by ourselves. In the meantime, we would skip ahead to the next section of coast unoccupied by firing ranges: the Dengie.

III

DENGIE

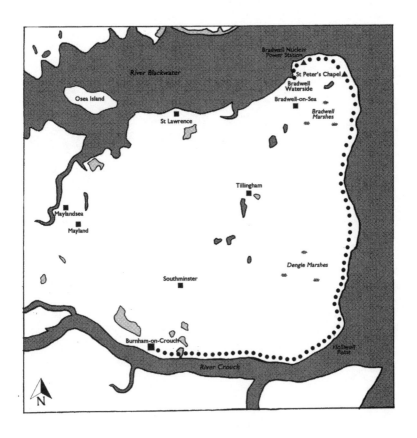

LATER THAT SPRING we made for the Dengie Peninsula, a flattened protrusion of land held between broad estuaries, the River Crouch to the south and the River Blackwater to the north. It is reputed to be the emptiest district in south-east England, the logical location for the closest nuclear power station to London, at Bradwell-on-Sea. Little more than an hour from London by direct train, we discovered a revelatory land of wide skies, long dykes and sea-walls.

We had first visited these marshes four years earlier, crossing the remotest country East Anglia could offer. Dengie is pronounced with a soft 'g', as we had discovered through trial and error, instantly exposing ourselves to the villagers of Bradwell as interlopers. There is nowhere to hide, for day-trippers such as ourselves or for anyone else, in a place as empty as the Dengie. Anyone who chooses to perch on the sea-wall at Tillingham Marshes with a pair of binoculars can monitor comings and goings over a five-mile sweep in every direction, including out to sea. It makes crossing the peninsula a strange experience in which the walker, entirely alone, nevertheless feels exposed and observed, as much by the landscape itself as by any creature within it.

Robert Macfarlane visited the Dengie for his book *The Wild Places*, searching for Britain's remaining wilderness. He lay on the sea-wall in a sleeping bag, watching the intersecting paths of migrating geese, gulls and airplanes on the approach to Stansted Airport, contemplating the myth of the sky-born wild hunt said to rush through the night sky in pursuit of deceased souls. The Dengie feels both ancient and ignored, a place that has been in endless, slow decline since the Romans pulled their legions out of Britain, sometime in the early 400s. Its isolation is exemplified by the lonely, barn-walled chapel of St Peter-on-the-Wall, once the object of a pilgrimage route that crossed Essex. The wall is the Dengie sea-wall, the most distinctive feature in the landscape for

miles around. St Peter's occupies the site of the lost Roman fort of Othona where St Cedd, a monk from Lindisfarne who brought Christianity to East Anglia, later founded what he described as his 'cathedral'. This too has become forgotten; its building was used as a barn until its restoration in the 1920s.

Spread between the Crouch and the Blackwater, with the North Sea shearing off its eastern edge, the peninsula is occupied by small villages and farms with names from deep antiquity: Dots and Melons Farm, Coney Hall, Bacons, Blackbirds, Munkins,

Twizzlefoot Bridge. Like much of the Essex coast, the Dengie consists of low-lying farmland drained by dykes and defended from the sea by a bank, lipped like the rim of a saucer. There is nothing quite like it, a slab of land 14 miles from north to south, sparsely populated, with an ancient chapel, a pair of Magnox nuclear reactors and, at least to the casual eye, little else.

To us it seemed a vulnerable place, with the ocean out of sight behind the embanked sea-wall, but impossible to forget. The Dengie is entirely dependent on this continuous barrier, a raised ribbon topped with a path that seals in the marshes. The entire Dengie was once saltmarsh and had been clawed back from the sea over several centuries. The Saxons grazed sheep on the saltings, but the 'law of the marsh' of 1210 established a collective obligation to maintain the sea defences and to encourage its conversion from sea to land. At some points nearby, where the sea-wall has been abandoned, archaeologists have discovered that the concrete and earth structures were built around medieval timber cores.

The medieval Essex marshes were known for their dairy produce, particularly the 'great and huge cheeses' described by John Norden in 1594, 'wondred at for their massivenes and thicknes.' Land reclamation only really took off in the 1600s when meat consumption grew and the Essex marshes became a convenient place to fatten livestock for sale in London. It was then that the Dutch arrived with their dyke-building skills. They knew a promising lowland when they saw it. Their expertise finally re-engineered the coastline, keeping the sea out and introducing a definitive separation between land and sea.

It was on that first visit to the Dengie, in 2012, that a plan to walk around the rest of Essex had germinated. Our day trip had provided the perfect antidote to a city obsessed with the London Olympics. The country felt obliged to celebrate something, but it was unclear what or why. Now, four years later, the Dengie called again. It promised refuge from a political atmosphere that was becoming fractious and confrontational. The EU referendum campaign was ushering marginal characters whose motivations were unclear into centre-stage. Nigel Farage was in the news every day, a scoundrel from a P.G. Wodehouse caper whose inevitable come-uppance never seemed to arrive. He had even been to Dulwich College, the same school as Wodehouse. Reality had been seamlessly replaced by parody, and no one seemed to mind. Boris Johnson, newly re-elected as an MP, had accused Barack Obama of encouraging Britain to remain in the EU through anti-British feeling, rooted in his Kenyan ancestry. This calculated cynicism, combining conspiracy theory with racist tropes, was unprecedented from a senior British politician in modern times.

We remembered the Dengie as a place ideal for acquiring

perspective: vast, spectacular in its loneliness and simplicity, just path, sea and sky. It was a place from a fever dream, its name suggesting a northern version of the tainted, dengue marshes of the Gulf Coast. John Norden, travelling in Essex in 1594, despite the 'manie and sweet commodeties' of the shire, complained about 'the Rochford, Denge, Tendering hundredes and other lowe places about the creekes, which gave me a moste cruell quarterne fever' (that is, a fever that flares up every fourth day). Daniel Defoe, in his *Tour Through the Whole Island of Great Britain*, reported that a 'strange decay of the sex' was found in the Dengie where young women, coming down from the uplands to marry farmers, succumbed to 'an ague'. This ague was common in the Essex marshes and is thought to have been malaria, spread by mosquitoes gathering around brackish water.

From the Middle Ages to the 19th century, ague was found in a few damp and low-lying areas of Britain, particularly the coastal marshes of Essex and Kent, the Lambeth and Westminster marshes in London, the Fens, the Somerset Levels and the Ribble Estuary in Lancashire. There is disagreement over whether this disease was malaria and, if so, how it reached Britain. Some claim it arrived in the 15th century, probably on ships from Africa and the east, while others believe it was endemic. It is difficult to be certain, as early records only referred to 'ague', a description encompassing many ailments. The malaria found in the marshes was not generally fatal but was highly debilitating, returning each year with the autumn rains and sometimes in the spring as well. It is thought to be one of the reasons for the sparse population found then, and now, in the marsh parishes of Essex.

Marsh fever disappeared from Essex only at the start of the 20th century, and it is suggested the respite could be short. Research predicts that the combination of increased travel and a warming climate could lead to malaria becoming endemic again in Britain. If it does, the coastal marshes would be the first place it would take hold. The first signs would be a sudden spread of a mysterious fever, unrecognised and untreated until it is too late.

We arrived one evening after work. The town faced the Crouch, where small sails rode at anchor against a backdrop of mudflats and a low, clear horizon. The waterfront was lined with timbered inns. On the quay, teenagers were gathered in a circle and chanting to a beat, their incantations drifting over the Crouch towards the far shore. We stayed in a room above a pub that had relaxed, along with the timbers holding it up, into obtuse angles.

Burnham-on-Crouch is a pretty and prosperous little town, its Georgian high street equipped with everything from a pocket cinema to a chandlery. In the early 1980s, Jonathan Raban had reported that the people of Burnham 'were fast and flash; they had fun, and they enjoyed letting other people see the colour of their money.' However, Burnham has none of the fake, neo-classical pediments and clock towers which mark out 1980s-boom Essex, and the flashness is probably confined to the yacht club bars. Burnham feels older and more confident, above the passing fashions.

The following morning, we walked out onto the quay and headed east. Jonathan Raban theorised that the unusual

'unhealthy but rich' Dengie landscape had created its own class system, with an absence of the landowning gentry found elsewhere in rural England. This left people more self-reliant, less dependent on landlords for permission, a culture he suggested had more in common with 'European peasants or American settlers'. Soon we passed the Royal Corinthian Yacht Club, a white, Modernist pavilion. Burnham is a yacht town, and the three clubs beside the river have long histories.

The Corinthian clubhouse is one of the few International

Style buildings in the UK. It had been designed for the 1932 Modern Architecture exhibition in New York by Joseph Emberton, who was also responsible for the exhibition halls at Olympia and Simpsons of Piccadilly. It was the epitome of the leisured 1920s and 1930s, when the expert sailors raised on the tricky mud channels of the Crouch turned their attention to regattas, races and cups. It was sailing weather, fine and clear with a light breeze stacking and dispersing towers of white cloud to the west. The yacht club was angular and impressive, an unexpected beacon of radical architecture gleaming across the Crouch.

We left the boats behind, except for a single sail which continued to match our walking pace for a full five miles, tracking alongside us. Then we left the dog walkers behind and, within 15 minutes of setting out, it was just us and the small boat tracking us out on the river. It would be five hours before we met another person. The path stretched out to a vanishing point, balanced and perfectly level on the crest of the sea-wall ringing the Dengie.

Walking soon became an act of weightlessness, and we felt suspended somewhere between land, sea and air. Time seemed to slow, as landmarks in the far distance not only refused to move closer as we marched towards them, but retreated in opposition to our steps. Ordinary features seemed to have become distorted, appearing larger than they were. The first five miles took us to

Holliwell Point, marked by what we were convinced was a Second World War fort, typical of the fortifications found all the way along this coast. By the time it had stopped shimmering on the horizon and assumed a settled shape, it had shifted and become a vast stack of bales 30 feet high, the tallest structure for miles around. A smaller stack had sunk into a rounded totem, deep shadows accentuated by raking light, with all the symbolic presence of a Paul Nash painting. This was no ordinary landscape.

To the south, on the far bank of the Crouch, two tall masts rose above land as flat as the Dengie itself. This was Foulness, home to the Shoeburyness Firing Ranges and accessible only to the army and to the few people who lived there. Something was not quite right about it. What seemed at first glance to be a church tower had a boxy look, as though the original had been replaced by a replica to deceive radar or to act as a target. Shapes on the Foulness horizon did not match recognisable structures, and we were unsure how to interpret what we saw.

The sea-wall path made a 90 degree turn to head due north from Holliwell Point. The rest of our journey lay ahead in a 10-mile-long straight line, terminating at St Peter's chapel. We turned towards the aspect of the Dengie that had changed since our last visit. Silhouetted against the wide sky were two groups of wind turbines, nine close by on Dengie Marshes, nine more to the north on Bradwell Marshes. We had asked about these on our previous visit, before they were constructed. The Bradwell resident we had spoken to had seemed philosophical, observing that the income from the turbines funded the village hall and that they would not be there for ever.

The turbines appeared both substantial and permanent. The largest structures for many miles, they dominated the marshes, their stiff shapes turning slow, sky cartwheels. They were like invading machines, striding out of the sea and inching towards nearby Maldon in an echo of *The War of the Worlds*, H.G. Wells' Martian invasion novel set on these very marshes. More turbines are on the way, with an application for a third group closer to Burnham. They could not be ignored, and there was no avoiding the Dengie's changed appearance since our first visit.

Wind turbines, however, were easier to remove than a nuclear power station. For the first time, Bradwell-on-Sea appeared as a grey, ghost box in the far distance. It was being decommissioned on a timescale that seemed to grow less certain every year. The marshes laid everything bare. In a place where there could be no hiding and even the ordinary seemed hyper-real, the presence of such outsized structures was unnerving.

Sir Henry Rider Haggard visited the Dengie in 1901. The author of high imperialist adventures, he was associated with the plains of southern Africa but lived across the border in Suffolk. In his self-appointed role as an agricultural reformer, he carried out a series of surveys of the state of rural England. He wrote of the Dengie, 'What must it be like when buried beneath the snows of winter, or when the howling easterly winds of spring sweep across its spaces, and the combers of the North Sea sometimes reach and batter their frail embankment. Then indeed I should not care to be the tenant of one of those solitary steads.' To Rider Haggard, the extremities of coastal Essex were as daunting and inhospitable as the far veldt.

Despite its remoteness, the Dengie conceals unsuspected connections. The Chelmsford Chronicle of 3rd October 1873 reported, 'We understand that large batches of Labourers have left the Dengie Hundred during the last few days for the North ... Any person travelling in the Dengie Hundred on Monday could hardly fail to notice wagon after wagon load of furniture going out or coming into this division of the County.' Three bad harvests in succession during the early 1870s had put pressure on work and wages in the Dengie, and migration north had been encouraged by the Agricultural Labourers' Union. Agents toured the Dengie villages speaking to large meetings of local workers in Burnham, Southminster, Steeple, Tillingham. They enthused about the benefits of leaving, even talking up Queensland as a place where wages were double those on offer in Essex. Emigration would also leave more work for those who remained at home. One union agent was reported to have proposed substituting a pig for a parson in each village, as a further social improvement.

Rather than Australia, the more appealing offer turned out to be higher pay for harder work in the collieries of the north-east. More than 250 people from the edge of Essex settled in the villages of County Durham. The largest group found their way to Butterknowle, a village in the coalfields. Sixty-two Dengie migrants were living there in 1881. Their new village was 20 miles from the coast, in the foothills of the Pennines. They would have encountered more contour lines walking to the local shop than in an entire Dengie lifetime.

Somewhere on the outskirts of Bridgewick Farm, I noticed that a five-bar gate across the sea-wall had been hung with high tide flotsam, arranged as offerings to placate something, or someone, somewhere. Caps, shoes, bread crates, milk containers, plastic balls and toys scoured from the foreshore had been tied to the gates in clusters. Single shoes – a black flip-flop, a white trainer with aubergine designs, a bedroom slipper – were bundled with bailer twine. A chewed plastic cartoon dog, stripped of its features, was perched on the top bar. A red, plastic beer crate hung from a manga-themed water bottle, a rusty bar thrust through its lattice. A wooden pole stood above it all, wearing a scarf and topped with a fat, greasy peaked cap, a scarecrow between jobs.

The strangeness of the marshes is lodged in modern popular culture. As well as H.G. Wells' Martians, who appeared from the North Sea off Foulness and stalked across the Dengie via the tiny village of Tillingham, Alfred Hitchcock was said to have taken inspiration from a visit to the marshes for his menacing film *The Birds*. Both had seen threat in the vastness of the sky pressing down on the land, the wide spaces open to the sea.

We spotted a distant line of people, the first since Burnham, gesturing rhythmically with white flags as they edged along the horizon like extras in *The Seventh Seal*. They were beaters, scurrying across a bean field to keep their line straight, as the dismal pop of shotguns plucked waterfowl from the sky. It had been reported locally that the Dengie was under surveillance as a suspected location for illegal hare coursing. With its isolation and long history of sport and game, this would surely be an ideal location but, with any human figure on the marshes visible for miles, it was hard to imagine how anything could be kept secret out here for long. Jonathan Raban closeted himself in a cottage on the Dengie in the early 1980s to write *Coasting*, his account of sailing around the coast of Britain. In a local pub he mentioned spotting a light aircraft more than once, landing in the dark. He 'was told sharply that it was best not to get too nosy about things one saw at night around the Dengie.'

As the sun sank lower we felt an increasing urge to reach our destination, the chapel of St Peter-on-the-Wall, and to leave the marshes before sunset. Night out here would be truly dark. As we approached the power station, and the chapel still hidden in trees, the dead straight line of the sea-wall became longer rather than shorter. The final mile stretched the furthest of all. Then we saw it, red-roofed with grey stone walls: the second-oldest working church in Britain, after St Martin's in Canterbury, founded in 653 by St Cedd, missionary to the East Saxons. The east is the Christian orientation – the direction of the rising sun and the risen Lord.

Cedd came as an ambassador of the Celtic Rite, an ascetic creed of personal denial practised by early monks, often within the walls of island monasteries. The site he chose was the abandoned Roman coastal fort of Othona, much of which had now disappeared under the sea. Its identity and purpose were eroded by time as well as water. The only written mention of Othona, during the latter days of Roman occupation, described it as garrisoned by a 'numerus fortensium', a 300-strong infantry unit 'of the brave'. It was marked on late 19th-century maps as 'Ethanchester', a spectral Roman town that seemed to have existed only in the cartographer's imagination. It was reported to be a 'huge ruin' in the 17th century. Its stones were thought to have been taken to build St Peter's.

The chapel is a very simple building – just a single, high space containing an altar. It has been used not only as a barn, but also as a military installation. St Peter's was part of a ring of coastal defences hastily thrown up in 1803 in response to Napoleon's promise to invade and subdue Britain. The ruined chapel was used as a semaphore station, its vantage point over the Dengie exploited to relay messages across the flat terrain using a system of jointed wooden arms. The system was sometimes described as the 'optical telegraph' which meant that you had to be able to see it to use it. The first news of a French invasion would have flashed across the Dengie, but only if the weather was clear.

In the days when travelling by water was much faster than on land, the Dengie was a stopping point on the North Sea trading routes linking Scandinavia, the Low Countries and the eastern seaboard of Britain. The North Sea was often known as the German Ocean, until the First World War swept German place names from our maps. Walking the empty 21st-century peninsula focused my mind on changes that had turned England in on itself and away from its once-connected edges. Jonathan Raban wrote that the people of the Dengie lived 'at an oblique angle to the rest of England.' In such an apparently isolated place, links to places beyond seem unlikely, yet its separation is to some extent a 20th century perspective. If the sea is viewed not as a border but a transport link, then northern Europe is not far away. But England is increasingly urbanised and centralised. Those places that once benefitted from proximity to Europe now find themselves cast aside by an economy that depends on flights to New York, Dubai, Shanghai. The Dengie may be out on its own but the rest of coastal Essex is not far behind. Being close to London's economy

does not guarantee benefits when London does business with international cities rather than its rural neighbours, and good rail connections make it as easy to leave as to stay.

Bradwell-on-Sea nuclear power station lay beyond, where the Dengie bulges north, surrounded by water on three sides. A pair of grey boxes squatting by the water. Like a northern mirage, they seemed to be connected both to the sea and the sheer cloud banks overhead. The power station was built on the site of RAF Bradwell Bay, a Second World War fighter base used to launch

attacks on airfields in occupied Europe and shipping off the Dutch coast. A single, mile-long runway remains south of the power station, still tarmacked, and aligned to the north-east, pointing across the North Sea towards the Frisian Islands.

Bradwell's location provided both the relative isolation from population centres and the endless amounts of water required for nuclear power. The reactor had opened in 1962, a shadowy presence whose arrival precipitated huge change for this remote marsh. Children's author Michael Morpurgo described the physical and psychological disruption caused by the arrival of a vast construction project in an undisturbed place in his book, *Homecoming*. The narrator, born in Bradwell, has no love for the grey hulks, describing them as 'a monstrous complex of building, rising from the marshes, malign and immovable.'

Bradwell was one of the UK's first nuclear power stations, construction starting in 1957. It was also one of the first to be decommissioned, closing in 2002. Magnox reactors were now only in operation in North Korea, and the decommissioning process had been underway ever since. It would last several decades. However, it was back in the news that week, as the new Prime Minister, Theresa May, delayed the decision on building new reactors at Hinkley Point C in Somerset. French and Chinese investment was proving hard to secure, the sums had never added up, and Bradwell was further down the same queue. Both the money and the reactor, the Hualong One, would be arriving from Beijing. Local opponents had staged a low-tide protest on the beach the previous year, but plans would later be confirmed for a 'Bradwell B' next door to the existing site. It would be the first Chinese reactor to be built in a developed country.

Raban suggested that, in the early days of Thatcherism at least, 'In the Dengie, people did things for themselves ... The place was a hive of tiny, tax-free private enterprises.' Researching the origins of the power station in advance, I had read a story about Bradwell, a theft with echoes of *Kiss Me Deadly*, the 1955 Robert Aldrich film noir. On 19th November 1966, police had stopped a van on the North Circular Road in London, suspecting that its steering was out of alignment. The driver was Dennis Hadley, a decorator from north London who worked at Bradwell Nuclear Power Station, and the van contained 20 natural uranium fuel rods. After Hadley was arrested it emerged that he and a rigger called Harold Sneath, from nearby Maylandsea, had broken into the fuel store and taken the rods. Hadley was on his way to sell them to a contact for scrap. Despite potentially disastrous consequences, avoided only by chance, the two were fined just £100 each on the basis that they had no idea what they were doing.

When we reached Bradwell, the end of this part of our journey, we needed transport to reach the nearest train station at Southminster, which was several miles back towards the Crouch. We visited two pubs in search of local information and a phone signal. At the first the welcome was frosty. The bar was dominated by three men who were discussing, loudly, the number of 'Pakis' in the England cricket team which, in their opinion, was too high. They brought us rapidly back to reality from our time on the sea-wall, and we felt slightly foolish to have felt, moments before, so mentally and physically separate from the everyday. In some ways the Dengie was like anywhere else, although overt, public racism has died out some time ago in the places in which we spent our time in London.

The second pub, fortunately, was friendlier. We had forgotten just how few people lived out here, and how few taxis were required to serve their needs. We systematically called every firm in east Essex, gradually realising how those located within sight on the opposite bank of the Blackwater were, in fact, a 40-minute drive around the estuary. Eventually we tracked down a ride from half way across the county, which took us to the cul-de-sacs of South Woodham Ferrers, a new town expansion completed in 1981. A BAE radar testing site on the summit of a hill overlooked the bypass as we drove in. The town was notable for streets named after characters from J.R.R. Tolkien's *The Hobbit*, including Gandalf's Ride, Gladden Fields, Meriadoc Drive and Thorin's Gate. They belonged to the newest part of town, an estate on the southern edge built in the 2000s, where Tolkien's fantasy version of a pre-war England had somehow become the real thing, although perhaps not quite the way the author had imagined it.

We left Essex feeling that we had visited deeply unfamiliar territory. The Dengie had repaid our expectations in full, just as remote and strange, shifting and otherworldly as its reputation suggested. It was harsh too, exposed and brittle. In such a flat setting, the least movement drew attention, and the impact of change was magnified. We had barely dented our 350-mile walk, but already we did not expect to find anywhere quite like this again.

IV

NORTHEY

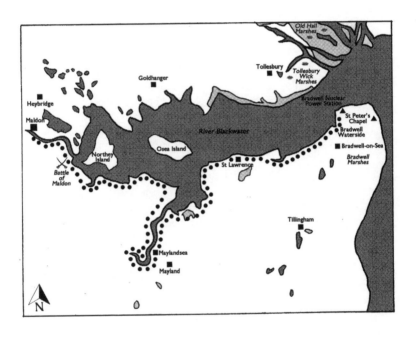

DURING THE SPRING OF 2016 we had little inkling of the cultural and political nervous breakdown just around the corner. The EU referendum votes in Britain and the presidential election in the USA were in the background of everyday events but everyone, including us, was confident they knew which way the tide was running. As we were to discover, the powerful and the influential had no idea what was coming. It was only in retrospect that we began to piece together the signs we had seen during our Essex walk: the shadow London of the Thames Estuary, home to casualised jobs and globalised logistics, subject to waves of failed regeneration, its poverty hidden in plain sight. Disconnection and discontent were in the air.

We returned to take up our walk where we had left off, at the village of Bradwell-on-Sea at the northern tip of the Dengie Peninsula, where the long Blackwater Estuary began. We boarded a weekend getaway train from Liverpool Street. The architectural historian Nikolaus Pevsner wrote that 'Essex is not as popular a touring or site-seeing county as it deserves to be ... due to the squalor of Liverpool Street Station.' Although written in 1954, Pevsner's opinion of the station has persisted and, even after its 1990s refurbishment, a layer of gloom remains over the platforms, beneath train shed roofs that could never be cleaned. Another ex-pat German, W.G. Sebald, was haunted by the atmosphere of the station and by the ghosts of his past. The Kindertransport route, which terminated at Liverpool Street, had brought children to London from Nazi Germany, saving them but not their families. The station approach enters a dark cutting through the East End, before delivering passengers at a destination with disturbingly little light.

In reverse, the journey is an opening out of skies and horizons, from the closely packed offices of the City to the wide air of the River Crouch. From our room in the same, sagging, timber-framed pub overlooking the Crouch, Wallasea Island could be made out on the opposite bank of the river. In a landscape dominated by skies, where solid ground seemed pancake-thin, the island appears only as a narrow band of darker horizon.

Wallasea is part of the Essex Archipelago, and the site of a strategic retreat in the face of the sea. The earth bored from beneath London during the construction of the Crossrail tunnels was transported to Wallasea in barges and used to reshape the coast. Three million tonnes of the capital's subsoil has been used to raise levels on parts of the island; the ultimate plan is to breach the sea-wall and create a landscape of saltmarsh and tidal islets. The RSPB, the organisation behind this coastal reshaping, is returning the land to a form last seen in the late Middle Ages, before the

Dutch engineers came to Essex. The project is forward-thinking and environmentally responsible, but at the same time there is a local feeling of unease about voluntarily giving land back to the sea.

We walked a little way upstream to find Bridgemarsh Island, hidden from Burnham by a bend in the Crouch. It looked like a long, dark smudge out on the river, a ghost island that had been lost despite the best efforts of its inhabitants. Farmed for centuries, it was large enough to have been divided between two parishes, Latching to the west and Althorne to the east. By the 1920s the sea had broken in at several points and the brick works was abandoned. Bridgemarsh Farm remained until the 1930s. In Jules Pretty's account, he describes how 'the island's final occupants, the Gooches, lived in the upper rooms of their lonely farmhouse as the tides washed through the ground floor twice a day.' These resolute, Canute-like farmers eventually left Bridgemarsh Island, but the land was used for grazing cattle and sheep until the Great Flood of 1953 penetrated the sea-wall and drowned the livestock. The island was abandoned and was now only a shadow visible in aerial photographs, still surrounded by a low and fatally incomplete sea-wall.

Wallasea survived the 1953 storm, and the many storms that had come before. Returning it to salt water was a good news story for environmentalists, but it was also an acknowledgment that a decline in farming, increased erosion and the inevitability of rising sea levels now made the status of land negotiable. The defences had already been opened and Wallasea was being reconfigured, revealing a previous forgotten topography. Without its defences, the island was separating into tidal islets again. The eastern end of the island, once called Canewdon, no longer existed. The RSPB described the land now being returned as having been 'borrowed' from the sea. Its return to water, as *The Guardian* put

it made 'mainland Britain just a little bit smaller.'

From Burnham we took a single-decker bus over the low farmland of the inner Dengie, through a band of villages sited on marginally higher ground above the marshes. We passed through Southminster, the final stop on the Crouch Valley branch line which connects the remote Dengie to the main railway at Shenfield. A town of only 4,000 people, Southminster seemed to me an unlikely place to have direct trains to London, but it owes its connection to the nuclear power station. While the Beeching

cuts closed branch lines across the country, including the line to Maldon at the head of the River Blackwater, the Crouch Valley line had national, strategic importance. Until 2006 it was used to transport flasks containing nuclear waste from Bradwell to Sellafield. Every Wednesday morning an 'up' train and a 'down' train on the single-track line were missing from the timetable, leaving room in the schedules for the nuclear cargo to pass through.

As the bus took us through Southminster I spotted an unusually large church. It was said to have Anglo-Saxon origins and, like St Peter-on-the-Wall, may have been founded by St Cedd. Its rector in the early 1800s, the Reverend Dr Alexander Scott, was chaplain and friend to Admiral Nelson on board HMS Victory, and sat with him below decks as he died, during the Battle of Trafalgar. The church's size may have had a bearing on its recreation by the ghost writer M.R. James as 'Southminster Cathedral' in his short story *An Episode of Cathedral History*. It recalls events of the 1840s when the cathedral was restored in Victorian Gothic style and the pulpit unwisely moved, releasing 'a moving form' with red eyes. The characters search the Bible for an explanation, but the best they can offer is that the apparition may have been a 'satyr'.

From Bradwell we intended to walk the southern shore

of the Blackwater Estuary to Maldon. At Maldon we would turn back out again along the northern bank of the river. The estuary is 10 miles long as the crow flies, but significantly more when every meander of the squirming coast path had been paced out. It would take a full two days of walking to reach Maldon and return to the same spot on the opposite bank, just a mile away across the water.

As its reactors wound down, the nuclear economy now employed fewer people, so Bradwell had pragmatically traded in its other assets. The former Bradwell Quay was now a marina, yacht club and sailing centre. We turned our backs on the sea for our day's walk west, heading inland with the broad Blackwater to the right, farmland to the left, and the sea-wall weaving precariously between. Arnold Bennett described the Blackwater as 'a true arm of the sea' with the changing moods of open water, and he was right. As we set off, it was a wide channel, the north bank forming a green-grey mirage rather than a firm skyline, and the yachts at sail out on the water changed colour with the sky.

West of Bradwell the sea-wall had been intentionally breached several years earlier; fields had been reflooded and returned to salt marsh. Five fields have been claimed by the Crouch. The Environment Agency has committed to 'holding the line' between Bradwell and St Lawrence, three miles west, for a further 10 years. After that, the landscape is up for grabs. The path skirted inland around the new marsh created by opening the levee, but returned to the coast at the caravans of the Waterside Holiday Park and the village of St Lawrence on a blunt peninsula. Until the early 20th century this had been Ramsey Island; The Wade, the channel that cut across the marsh separating it from the mainland, has since been closed.

We entered St Lawrence on a path along the backs of houses, which were boat-shed bungalows built as the mid-20th century boom charged the Essex economy and scattered inner Londoners into its far periphery. Its waterfront was called The Stone and was much older – a landing place which, with its pub and oyster beds, had formed the entirety of the village 100 years before. A sailing club now occupied the beds and a pink smiley flag flew on the point, as though transmitting a subversive code to the passing yachts.

On the point, beside the massed blue, pink and white sheets of the Marconi Sailing Club, was a lawn with an Edwardian house in the distance. The sailing club had been set up in the 1950s for employees of Marconi wireless and radar factory at Chelmsford. The chance of some sailing on the Blackwater must have been a powerful incentive to work hard. The house was Stansgate Hall Farm, home of the Benn family. It was first acquired by William Wedgwood Benn, a Liberal MP who joined the Labour party in the 1920s, before becoming a Labour peer and a minister in the Attlee government.

His son, Tony Benn, inherited the title Viscount Stansgate when his father died in 1960. He was an MP at the time, and his new title immediately disqualified him from sitting in the House of Commons. He stood at the subsequent by-election anyway, in protest, and instigated a change in the law which allowed him, and all future inheritors of unwanted peerages, to renounce his title and regain his seat. His Conservative opponent, who had been automatically granted his seat, returned it to him. Benn did, however, hold on to Stansgate Hall Farm and he lived there until his death in 2014. He died just before the unexpected revival in the Labour Left, of which he was the unofficial leader for many years. His obituaries characterised him as a representative of a lost politics, safely consigned to the past by Neil Kinnock and then Tony Blair, and his death fuelled nostalgia for a time now gone. Astonishingly, it was only a year later that his spiritual successor, Jeremy Corbyn, the least likely person ever to wield power in the Labour party, was elected leader. Benn's long exile on the political and physical periphery suddenly felt like preparation rather than a retreat. The political profile of Essex was more complex than generally imagined, conducive to a maverick individualism that connected to the left as well as the right, spawning both collective experiment and mass conformity.

From the long lawns of Stansgate, we suddenly emerged into Steeple Bay Holiday Park, which was static caravan and jet ski territory. The machines spouted and barked, scoring wakes across the sheltered inlet and out onto the Blackwater. At high tide, Mayland Creek seemed to stretch impossibly far, washing over acres of what the map insisted was land, but which appeared to be currently under water. Plovers dipped and dived, with cries

that, as J.A. Baker had pointed out, were easily confused with the peewit – the northern lapwing. A high background 'peee-wit' was the estuary soundtrack.

The entire landscape had settled down to mud level, leaving only the sea-wall high and dry. Mayland and Maylandsea, two conjoined villages, appeared covertly prosperous. Inconspicuous at the foot of the deep, shifting creek, a small gridiron of dead-straight 1960s avenues led us to a marina and a row of waterfront villas, which seemed perfect hideaways. The cars parked in

generous drives were high-end. In one of the most isolated villages in the south-east, a silver BMW coupé was a standard accessory, ideal for eating up the long Dengie lanes. We could see there was no sign of the Cardnells yard, where torpedo boats had been manufactured.

The Ordnance Survey map records an unusually large area of glasshouses at Mayland, which proved, on inspection, to be no longer there. As Ken Worpole notes, they were demolished in 2013. However, the land which had once contained them remained divided into long, narrow garden strips, either side of the lane which leads to Mayland Creek and the remains of the Pigeon Dock landing stage. This was the site of the Great Experiment, 'today a collection of abandoned outhouses, overgrown glasshouses, former railway tracks, and river piers.' Mayland had been a socialist colony, an experiment in alternative living set up by a Manchester printer, Thomas Smith, who moved south in 1895. Rather than encouraging a traditional return to the soil, the community became known for its use of pioneering scientific farming techniques, including the use of glasshouses.

Six hundred acres of farmland were made available as smallholdings to families wanting to escape the city and regain control of their lives. The Great Experiment attracted visits from socialist thinkers of the time, including Beatrice and Sidney

Webb, Keir Hardie and George Lansbury. It also attracted, perhaps unsurprisingly, a visit from H. Rider Haggard wearing his agricultural reformer hat. The Mayland Colony came to an end in 1914, but some of the smallholders bought their plots and stayed on, giving the landscape a profile entirely distinct from the surrounding farms.

During the first half of the 20th century, anarchist and socialist thinking led to experiments in living with the aim of achieving separation from the constraining, oppressive systems of capitalism. Two contrasting approaches were influential in Essex, created by a pair of big-bearded Russian intellectuals. Anarchist communism was devised by Peter Kropotkin, who had visited Mayland. He advocated a decentralised form of communism, self-organising in preparation for the coming collapse of capitalism. The author Leo Tolstoy, on the other hand, had developed an anarcho-Christian doctrine of his own, based on pacifism and individual change, which would lead to social transformation. These theories were put into practice on a micro scale by a series of small communities, each practising its own version of the future. Mayland was one of several such 'colonies' in Essex at the turn of the 20th century. Others included the Tolstoyan anarchist settlements set up at Purleigh, Ashingdon and Wickford in the 1890s, which attempted to promote communal living.

George Lansbury, later leader of the Labour party, was inspired by Mayland into founding a socialist colony at Laindon Farm, outside Basildon, in 1904.

The colonies arrived at a particularly fertile time for alternative conceptions of society. Their rise accompanied the unprecedented changes brought about by industrialisation, and was fuelled by the social upheaval of the First World War. A remarkably high proportion of the leading intellectual figures of the time were actively involved in pursuing the creation of new social orders, away from the unsustainable decay they witnessed in the industrial cities. One hundred years later, it is particularly striking how seriously the idea of living in new ways was taken, by politicians, planners, writers and artists. From D.H. Lawrence to Rabindranath Tagore, H.G. Wells to Patrick Geddes, Rider Haggard to Lansbury; people with wildly different political philosophies were not only dreaming of new and better worlds, they were actually attempting to set them up. The combination of naivety and vision involved in remaking social relations seems both culturally distant and quite enviable.

The path wound around the saltings, then crossed into an empty quarter. Dead flat, a steep sea embankment sealed the estuary from acid-yellow rapeseed fields in the middle distance. From the top, the vista over the Blackwater took in the opposite bank, two miles away, apparently uninhabited. All the action was on the river, boats under sail passing between Maldon and the North Sea. The ghostly forms of topsail barges tacked along the river's roads, their full sheets moving from dark red to black as clouds slid over.

I had been reading an essential text, beloved of landscape writers, which promised to peer deep into the interior of Essex. The Blackwater Estuary was J.A. Baker territory. Baker achieved unlikely fame in 1968 with the publication of his luminous Essex nature book *The Peregrine*. He lived in Chelmsford and roamed the fields and marshes to the east, along the Blackwater and the Dengie. Baker was no ordinary writer and *The Peregrine*, one of only two books he published, is widely lauded as one of the greatest pieces of landscape writing in English. He followed peregrine falcons obsessively across the countryside of south-east Essex for many years. At first, he worked in a series of menial jobs, including pushing trolleys in the British Library. Eventually, he gave up conventional life to spend as much of his time as possible in the wild. *The Peregrine* records, in hallucinatory detail, a single season in his pursuit of the bird, from October 1963 to April 1964. Throughout that winter, a particularly harsh one, Baker walked out in all weathers to follow the magnificent raptors as they hunted across their marshland territory. At the time he was writing, the dominion of DDT threatened to wipe out wildlife at the top of the food chain, and the peregrine was particularly threatened. Baker was convinced he was observing the last peregrines and that they were doomed to become extinct. In fact, after his death in the early 1980s, the peregrine made a remarkable recovery. The book is an intensely personal account, but consists almost entirely of observation and description of landscape and wildlife – the behaviour of birds and their relationship to the world around them. In fact, these accounts are inseparable from

Baker who, in his attempts to make himself disappear into his surroundings to track the peregrines, becomes more visible as he merges with his subject.

Baker's author biography reads, 'John Baker is in his forties and lives with his wife in Essex. He has no telephone and rarely goes out socially.' *The Peregrine* is dedicated 'To my Wife', but she does not otherwise feature in the book. Her shadowy presence in the endpapers gives the only layer of perspective to the book outside Baker's narrow, piercing focus. As he pursues

the peregrines, he becomes more and more like them, wary of humans, whom he sees only in raptor terms as a threat. His vision of the Essex coast becomes increasingly dreamlike: 'I will follow him until my predatory human shape no longer darkens in terror the shaken kaleidoscope of colour that stains the deep fovea of his brilliant eye. My pagan head shall sink into the winter land, and there be purified.' *The Peregrine* is not only the most compelling nature book I have read; it is also the most terrifying. The flat lands of Essex contain life and death in unchanged, primal forms. Baker's communion with the wild took him across a boundary that few could see, nevermind cross, into a world of intense beauty and unending horror. The two could not be separated.

To the west the Blackwater channel narrows, splitting into two creeks as it approaches Maldon, passing either side of Northey Island. The sea defences that have kept the island dry are no longer intact. The sea-wall was breached during the Great Flood of 1953 and the defences on the west side of the island washed away. Today, three quarters of the island has returned to the sea. The tumulus marked on maps at the northern tip of the island is now inaccessible, submerged under the saltings.

Owned by the National Trust, the island can only be reached, with their permission, via a tidal causeway across Southey

Creek. Our timing was poor; we surveyed Northey from the far side of a saltwater channel, but our failure to cross the water felt appropriate. This is a site of great symbolic importance in the history of England, the location of the Battle of Maldon, fought on 11th August 991AD at the landward end of the causeway leading to the island. The battle, between the Saxon men of Essex led by Earl Byrhtnoth and invading Vikings under the Norwegian Olaf Tryggvason, is the subject of one of the oldest surviving poems in English. The anonymous, incomplete poem tells how the Viking raiders, having sailed up the Blackwater and landed on Northey Island, were trapped at the causeway by Byrhtnoth's men. They demanded gold and armour in return for leaving. Byrhtnoth refused. The tide, which 'came flowing, flood after ebb', or 'flod æfter ebban' in the original poem, kept the armies apart. But the earl's sense of pride led him into a fatal error. He allowed the Viking forces, at their request, to cross the causeway to the mainland for a fair fight. The 'sea robbers' broke the Saxon shield wall and three men hacked Byrhtnoth down beneath eagles and ravens 'eager for carrion'. The eagles and ravens had departed but the battle site, under an arching, grey Essex sky, remained sombre.

The first evidence of Maldon itself was the Marine Parade Recreation Ground, a busy park on the edge of the town. As we walked through the park, a group of teenagers were driving an ageing Volvo slowly up and down the playing field, hanging out of the windows and climbing on the roof. No one paid much attention when one, misjudging a leap, kicked out the windscreen. Families were buying ice cream at the end of a long café queue, and children were racing along the riverfront. The sea bathing pool had been closed ever since, we were later told, a man had drowned there some years earlier.

Maldon's real centre is not the high street at the top of the hill but the Hythe (meaning 'landing place') at its foot, where the town meets the river. Here pubs and boatyards jostle on the wharf, the solidity of the hard contrasting with the soft mud shaped by the retreating tides, every edge rubbed away to leave only smooth, sinuous, treacherous forms. A rake-thin, sword-wielding bronze statue of Byrhtnoth commands the river. The persistent English character myth of the gallant but honourable loser has a counterpart in another Essex battle. The Battle of Assandune was said to have been fought in 1016, on the Crouch at Ashingdon, in the Essex Archipelago, between Edmund Ironside and the Danish prince Canute. The English harried the invading Danes as they advanced through Essex, but were eventually defeated in battle, said to have been betrayed by one of their own men. The battle completed the Danish conquest of all England outside Wessex.

Maldon is the home port for the red-sailed barges, which

had returned from their estuary trips and were lined up along the quay. These, we discovered, are Thames sailing barges – flat-bottomed boats designed to work the tidal estuaries of the Thames and the Medway. Capable of operating in as little as three feet of water, the barges once carried all manner of goods upstream and downstream between the Essex quays and the London Docks. They were redundant by the end of the 1960s, with the final trip under sail in 1970, carrying cattle cake from Tilbury to Ipswich. The Cook's Yard fleet, which had operated since the 1890s, now ran tourist outings from Maldon. A flotilla of barges crossed the English Channel to help evacuate the British Expeditionary Force from Dunkirk in 1940. The barges were also raced in the Thames Match, which was set up in the 1860s and has run, intermittently, ever since. The race begins at Tilbury, leading out along the Thames Estuary and back to Gravesend, and is said to be the second oldest sailing race in the world after the America's Cup.

As we climbed the hill into Maldon, the town revealed itself to be handsome, with flint-spired churches, a Georgian high street and a pocket-sized town hall. The Blue Boar, a big coaching inn with a gateway large enough for the most flamboyant of coaches, was flying a red 'Vote Leave' flag on a pole outside – like a national flag. This was the first Leave campaigning material we had seen anywhere since the referendum campaign had begun.

This public declaration was a jolt to our complacency. We realised what should have been obvious, that Leave had no need to campaign here. It was simply proclaiming the collective view over the pretty rooftops.

Maldon was built with a confident architecture born of the long years of prosperity from its position at the head of the Blackwater. Its high street was elegant, but seemed now to be in an economic trough. Poverty was apparent among the passers-by. A man in a dirty coat was waiting for the Salvation Army shop to close so he could settle down in its doorway. It was Saturday evening, but the town was quiet. The only noise came from a posse of young men and women carrying a huge set of speakers on their shoulders, strutting down the middle of the road in a bubble of UK garage. They carried a cultivated air of menace, but Maldon did not seem to notice as they passed through. Their shouts echoed along the narrow, 18th-century side streets as they marauded back to the station to catch the last train out of the marshes. We spent the night in a B&B – as Georgian as the rest of Maldon – where the owner claimed that groups came down from Basildon every weekend, like a residual army of invading Vikings still keeping the coastal towns honest 1,200 years on.

V

BLACKWATER

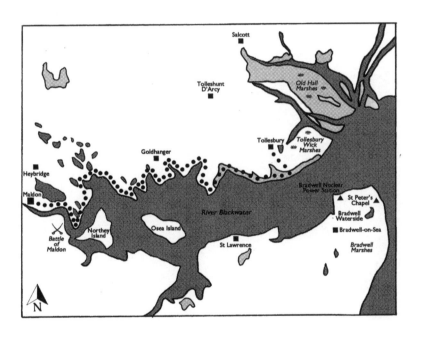

IT WAS JUNE by the time we returned to Maldon, anxious to continue our exploration along the low-lying north bank of the Blackwater. We had watched it from the south bank under changing light during several hours of walking and it seemed mysterious and empty. This was real marsh country, I thought. Maldon lies at the confluence of the River Blackwater and the River Chelmer, both of which flow only in Essex from source to sea. Maldon is connected to the foundation history of England. The resistance of Byrhtnoth and his band of East Saxons was part of a stock of stories on which concepts of England as a distinct culture has been built. On the east coast of England, gaping river estuaries invited visitors from across the North Sea to anchor, raid and settle.

The England cricket captain at the time of our walk, Alastair Cook, is a Maldon man. Cook is associated with the traditional cricketing values of patience and concentration, his batting out of joint with the times, and you would not find him clearing the boundary for bonuses in the Indian Premier League or the Australian Big Bash. In 2015, Cook passed his Essex mentor, Graham Gooch, as the leading run scorer for England in Test cricket. The team's fortunes seemed to ebb and flow with Cook's form, peaking when he was at the top of his game, dragged into introspection when he scratched around for elusive runs. At his lowest points he was famous for retreating to his farm to help with the lambing and get his head together.

Intriguingly, there was also a genuine Marvel superhero from Maldon. In the late 1970s Marvel Comics introduced Captain Britain, dressed in a Union Jack skinsuit and wielding a quarterstaff, a transparently retooled version of Captain America. His backstory was in Maldon as Brian Braddock, raised by aristocratic parents (Sir James and Lady Elizabeth) who were down on their luck, but living in a Tudor manor with a research lab in the basement. After a series of unfortunate events, Brian became protector of the nation, Captain Britain, under the guidance of Merlyn. This unconvincing selection of myths was rebooted by Northampton comic master Alan Moore, who systematically destroyed Captain Britain's grip on reality, flicking between parallel universes featuring alternative versions – Captain Albion, Captain England, Captain UK – as he moved towards a new mythology in which superheroes were the most flawed characters of them all.

On a Saturday morning, Maldon was busy with plant sales, weekly shops and pub coffees. We stopped outside All Saint's Church in the centre of the town and scrutinised its triangular church tower, a style unique in Britain and built for reasons that were no longer understood. I noticed statues of

St Cedd and Byrhtnoth standing guard above the main door. The church contained an unexpected commemoration of links between Great Britain and the United States: the Washington Window, installed in memory of George Washington's great-great-grandfather Laurence, who had been Rector of Purleigh, deep in the Dengie Peninsula, during the English Civil War. The window was given by the citizens of Malden [*sic*], Massachusetts in 1924 as a commemoration of the bonds across the Atlantic between two 'Anglo-Saxon cultures'. It features the figures of three saints representing Patriotism, Freedom and Colonisation.

The church had belonged to Beeleigh Abbey on the outskirts of Maldon, which was built in 1180 for an order of monks from northern France called the Norbertines, or 'White Canons'. The Abbey was once a pilgrimage site, home to the heart of Roger Niger, a 12th-century Bishop of London with Essex connections. It was said that his burial caused an eclipse of the sun. He became an unofficial saint, and the Abbey a medieval pilgrimage site. Later, the pilgrimages continued for different reasons. A 16th-century house was built around the abbey buildings, and was the home of fearsome bookshop proprietor Christina Foyle until her death in 1999. Employees at Foyles, her chaotic emporium on Charing Cross Road, were invited for nerve-wracking weekend visits to Beeleigh, where they were inspected. Back at Foyle's, a famously complicated checkout system involved queuing twice, in two different parts of the shop, while Foyles' indifference to stocktaking made it the place to find books no other shop had stocked for decades.

Walking out of Maldon to the north, we crossed the Chelmer and then the Chelmer and Blackwater Navigation, taking the towpath back towards salt water. Across the river we entered Heybridge, the Maldon's industrial twin, a separate village which had consented to the canal its neighbour did not want. It

had the rough end of the deal. The dominant Bentall's agricultural machinery factory beside the river had closed at the end of the 1980s. Its name now belonged to a shopping centre with an Asda supermarket in distinctive 1980s out-of-town style, with pitched roof and non-functional clock tower. It looked like a snide parody of the 18th-century grandeur of Maldon High Street.

The fringe politics of the Essex coast were also lurking here. Later in the year, it was reported that Heybridge Parish Council had been taken over by the BNP, who fielded candidates

under the banner 'Fighting Unsustainable Housing Because We Care.' As parish council politics was usually non-aligned and seats often uncontested, this subterfuge seemed like the convulsions of a dying party whose best option was to pretend it was something else. However, the BNP's aggressive anti-immigration stance, based unashamedly on prejudice rather than facts, had undoubtedly entered mainstream debate, enabled by UKIP, right-wing media outlets and the anti-European wing of the Conservative party. Two years later, the BNP's only parish council was still in place.

The route down to the estuary led along the final stretch of the Chelmer and Blackwater Navigation. This waterway was built to connect the county town of Chelmsford, 13 miles away, to the sea. It stopped taking commercial traffic in 1972, and the gravel pits at its mouth are now lakes surrounded by very new, redbrick houses. A sea lock releases the Blackwater into the wide expanse of its estuary. This was once a well-used route for materials travelling across the North Sea and up and down the coast, when water was a connection rather than a barrier and when the coast was the centre as well as the edge.

H.G. Wells, who rented a house in the Essex countryside, knew Maldon and saw it as an escape route. In *The War of the Worlds*, the narrator's relatives flee the country by boarding a ship at Maldon bound for Ostend. In scenes which prefigured the Dunkirk evacuation, boats of all sizes swarmed along the Essex coast and filled the Blackwater Estuary: '[S]team launches from the Thames, yachts, electric boats ... ships of large burden, a multitude of filthy colliers, trim merchantmen, cattle ships, passenger boats, petroleum tanks, ocean tramps, an old white transport even, neat white and grey liners from Southampton and Hamburg.' As the transports streamed into the North Sea, Martian heat rays destroy the navy's ironclad, 'Thunder Child', in full view of the Essex shore.

We were soon on the north bank of the river, looking back across the tidal mudscape towards the Hythe at Maldon. At low tide the estuary at Maldon is an oozing landscape of channel-riven mud, appearing every inch the type of landscape that would swallow a grown man whole. Maldon has embraced its slimy setting and founded a new annual tradition, the Mud Race. The race began in the early 1970s as a swim and stumble through the wide mudflats at the mouth of the Blackwater, where a barrel of beer awaited the winner on the opposite bank. The beer has disappeared, but the race continues. Essex tourism posters at Liverpool Street Station advertise it as a quirky attraction, hoping to entice commuters off-route and into the badlands of Essex. Anyone who does so will see a small crowd dragging themselves on their hands and knees across the estuary at low tide in mud-drenched costumes, immersing themselves in a medium that is neither land nor sea.

Heybridge Basin mirrors the Hythe in Maldon: a quayside of pubs and pleasure boats. We walked the narrow cement lip that separates land from sea and surveyed the wide channels of the Blackwater. The north side of Northey Island was now visible in the estuary, and I glimpsed Northey House among trees, perched on a nub of land that remained above sea level. Between 1923 and the Second World War, this was the home of Sir Norman Angell. Angell designed the house, the only one on the island. A journalist, Labour MP, political theorist and international peace campaigner, Angell had roamed the world, working as a cowboy in 1890s California and as a journalist on the continent, eventually becoming Paris Editor of *The Daily Mail*. He was knighted, and received the Nobel Peace Prize in 1933, the only person to be thus honoured for publishing a book. *The Grand Illusion*, released in 1910, had proposed a theory for the end of war. It explored the idea that the financial and business links between major powers meant that war was no longer in any country's interests. Unfortunately, his theory was proved wrong over and over again. Jean Renoir's First World War film *La Grande Illusion* is a powerful riposte, delivered as Europe descended into the turmoil of the Second World War. Angell died in the late 1960s, having witnessed successive international failures to place peace above national interest.

Angell had bought Northey Island from Vierville de Crespigny, a local eccentric who was probably sent to live there in internal exile to save his family embarrassment. De Crespigny was obsessed with the Irish, whom he believed might invade at any moment, and spent much of his time, armed, patrolling the island in a purpose-designed hut on wheels to cover likely landing spots. In my mind, the name Blackwater carries invasion associations beyond the Essex coast. A private military contractor called Blackwater Security Consulting was employed by the US government to protect government convoys in Iraq during the years following the 2003 invasion. In this capacity, Blackwater employees were responsible for the 2007 Nisour Square massacre in Baghdad, in which 17 Iraqi civilians were killed during a firefight with the police. Three Blackwater employees were convicted of manslaughter and another of murder, a verdict which was subsequently overturned after 10 years of court challenges. The intense publicity that resulted encouraged Blackwater to change its name, and it is now known as Academi.

Long grasses brushed our legs as we pushed out along the sea-wall, and laid a coating of pollen on our walking trousers. Out on the estuary, a slab of land had separated itself from the horizon and was moving closer as we walked. This was Osea Island, larger and more intact than Northey, having survived the 1953 storm surge and retained its sea-wall. Osea was a place of many identities. Its name was thought to be Danish, but the Romans had occupied the island and left behind evidence of intensive pottery production. Seven hundred years later a number of Earl Byrhtnoth's men were buried, according to contemporaries, on the island.

Osea can only be reached from the far bank via a tidal causeway which crosses a mudflat called The Stumble. Casual visitors are not welcome. While Northey Island is now owned by the National Trust, Osea is a private island, having been bought in 2000 by Sugababes' producer Nigel Frieda. It is best known as the home of an alcohol and drug rehabilitation centre, a retreat for the wealthy and famous. The ultra-conservative writer James Wentworth Day visited in 1949 and 'found only a farm and a home for inebriates', but he imagined something else too: 'The cradle of

English history.' Tying together Osea and Northey, he claimed 'This river and these two islands saw the forging of our England.' More recently, residents on Osea have included the doomed soul diva Amy Winehouse. The centre was set up in 1903 by brewery heir Frederick Charrington, after a visionary conversion to temperance. He sold his shares in the family business, apparently after witnessing a man beating his wife outside a Charrington's pub as she begged him to come home, and used the money to campaign for temperance. The Causeway Retreat was heavily fined in 2010 after an inspection revealed 'standards that would shame a third world country'. The island was now advertised as 'the UK's leading retreat for the music industry', with recording studio and accommodation for 'your next party destination'. It is only 20 minutes by helicopter from Battersea Helipad in London.

Osea is surrounded by an aura of exclusion and mystery, and it was no surprise to discover from the owner of our Maldon B&B that it had been used as a secret naval base during the First World War. The remains of a military railway were apparently still visible on the island, a line built during the development of a new, fast and lightweight torpedo boat called the Coastal Motor Boat. It came into service at the end of the war, sinking a German destroyer across the North Sea in Zeebrugge and a Soviet Russian ship in the Baltic.

Osea was one of the last remaining habitats of the raven in south-east England, from where it had disappeared in the late 19th century. In January 1890, the Essex Field Club reported that ravens had been seen on Osea Island, but that 'the Raven is already trembling on the very verge of extinction in Essex'. Ravens had been poisoned and shot by farmers protecting their lambs, and branches on which they nested on cut down. The raven has a bad reputation, as a bird of ill omen and a scavenger of the dead, as recorded in 'The Battle of Maldon'.

Carl Jung took up the raven's cause claiming that it represented the shadow side of the psyche – the part of us we do not see, but which contains essential energies. The raven also lies at the heart of another English foundation myth, as a guardian of wisdom. The ravens of the Tower of London were specially chosen to guard the head of Brân, the mythical Celtic King of England who is buried beneath the White Tower, and to protect his memories while he sleeps. In the early 2010s, ravens were bred in England for the first time in 120 years, on the White Cliffs at Dover, having spread slowly back from their redoubts in the north and west. It has even been suggested that they could eventually return to the marshes.

The landscape of the Blackwater is marked by the long-dead and appealed to M.R. James. He set his ghost story *The Rose*

Garden in a fictional parish outside Maldon. An upper-middle-class couple, the Anstruthers, spend their time on golf and charitable works. Mrs Anstruther is keen to plant a rose garden and unwisely overrides her gardener's reluctance to uproot a large post that lies in the way. It happens to be on a spot where people feel 'the most intense anxiety, oppression and hopelessness.' It turns out the post was placed there by clergymen in the late 17th century after locals were 'troubled' following a death. The post is removed, and Mrs Anstruther sees a face at the window that gives her such a severe shock that it is 'decided that she must spend the winter abroad.'

Outside Goldhanger we saw a distant crowd of fruit-pickers, working their way across the fields below our elevated route along the sea-wall. They wore colourful headscarves and, from a distance, looked eastern European. They were picking strawberries. Bounds Farms at Goldhanger is the site of the specialist strawberry fields of jam producers Wilkin and Sons of Tiptree, and the tiny, prized Little Scarlet fruit is grown here. Little Scarlet strawberries are temperamental, but both small and valued for remaining intact in the jar. 'Did you know that Little Scarlet is James Bond's favourite conserve?' enthuses the Tiptree catalogue.

Wilkins and Sons was founded in 1885 as the Britannia

Fruit Preserving Company. Little Scarlet Conserve was indeed mentioned in Ian Fleming's novel *From Russia With Love*, alongside Cooper's Vintage Oxford Marmalade, in several paragraphs of aggressively precise directions on Bond's breakfast requirements ('his favourite meal of the day'). He took his breakfast while trying to work out why he felt lethargic, recalling vaguely that he was upset because his lover had left him.

In 2016, the title of Fastest Picker in the annual Tiptree Strawberry Race, held at Bounds Farm, went to a Polish picker, with a Romanian as runner-up. That year's race was held in honour of the Queen's 90th birthday and the competitors wore what Colchester's *Daily Gazette* described as 'royal dress'. On the Wilkin & Sons website, a page headed 'Modern Slavery Statement' hints to a darker side to the industry.

We turned off the sea-wall into Goldhanger village, where an entire bungalow was decorated with a giant 'Get Britain Out' poster. Another neighbouring bungalow displayed a tiny, perfect model of the nearby flint church on its front lawn. In 1865, Lewis Carroll stayed at Goldhanger Rectory, where he was reported to have heard a comical story which claimed that treacle pits had formed in Goldhanger after consignments of sugar beet had been left to dissolve. In *Alice in Wonderland*, the Dormouse tells Alice a story about three sisters who lived in the bottom of a well, subsisting on treacle. Sweetness comes out of the ground here.

Past Goldhanger, we walked out into a landscape that seemed truly wild to us, almost paralysing in the sheer volume of sky and the spread of the long, low horizon. The north bank of the Blackwater was empty apart from the occasional farm in the middle distance among low trees. I had checked pre-war maps of the area to understand whether it had always been like this. They had showed an extraordinary object: a pond shaped like an eight-armed wheel of fire, paused in an anti-clockwise

spin, trailing sparks. It had been filled and ploughed during the Second World War, but aerial photographs revealed a dark after-image burned into the corn. Despite its remarkable appearance, this was a standard design for a duck decoy pond. Invented by the Dutch, they once lined this bank of the estuary, wildfowling territory where duck, teal and wigeon were hunted for sale in the markets of London. The ponds were screened with vegetation and exploited the natural curiosity of ducks, which like to keep predators in sight. They could be lured into the narrow, netted

arms of the pond by a dog, trained to show itself at gaps in the bushes, or by a man laying a trail of grain.

The Blackwater was known for its decoy ponds in the 18th and 19th centuries, and also for its punt guns. These fearsome weapons were mounted on flat-bottomed boats which could glide among the reeds towards the feeding grounds for flocks of water birds. In 1904 Harry Handley of Maldon recalled killing 432 dunlin with a single shot while punting at Stansgate Abbey Farm, on the south bank of the Blackwater. This seems scarcely credible, but I discovered several other reports that punt-gunners had often killed hundreds of birds with a single discharge of their weapons on the Blackwater and Dengie marshes.

From our vantage point on the sea-wall, we could see occasional mounds inland among the fields and dykes. We pushed across the six miles of marsh separating us from our destination, the village of Tollesbury. The map marked nine 'red hills' along our route, the piled remnants of Bronze Age salt pans. The ancient mounds were hardly discernible as hills, but left a red smear of clay on the blackish soil. These are mysterious features of the East Anglian coast, found particularly in Essex, and their purpose has only been discovered in the last few decades. They are clay-lined pits used to store sea water, which was heated on clay trays to evaporate sea salt. Salt was a valuable commodity, and these red hills were the first signs of a vigorous trade based on the Essex coast. The Domesday Book records hundreds of salt pans across the county. More than 2,000 years later, Essex is still known for its sea salt, which is harvested from the saltings around Maldon and sold by the Maldon Salt Company. At home in the 1980s, the Maldon box, with its mineral taste of the shore, was specifically reserved for sprinkling on baked potatoes.

Hay fever season had arrived, and the sea-wall path was an increasingly wild tangle of long grass. The pollen was now drifting in the air, flicked up with every touch, and laying pale dust over us as we brushed through. It was a hay fever nightmare and Jo, whose symptoms are usually fairly mild, had become increasingly agitated since we left Heybridge, some eight miles back. Her eyes were now so swollen that she was having problems seeing. The marshes were summer-green, and the estuary glinted in the sun, but the landscape was turning hostile. We were anxious to reach the end of our journey and escape the miasma. There was even more remote marshland ahead of us, but it would take another day of walking to make our way around the twin spurs of the Tollesbury and Old Hall marshes which reached out towards Mersea Island.

In this allergen fug, we passed the site of Tollesbury Pier, reduced to a grassy strip across the saltings. The pier, once served by the lost Crab and Winkle Line railway, had been a failed attempt to jump-start the tourist trade, ferrying visitors out to the yachting country of the Blackwater Estuary. The railway was extended from the village to the pier to unlock the remote coast for holiday trade, but was not the success it had been anticipated to be. It was requisitioned by the army during the First World War and the pier blown up during the Second, to strengthen the porous Essex coastline. The route closed in 1951 due to lack of traffic, but the railway continued to carry soft fruit to the Wilkin and Sons jam factory until the 1960s.

As our path turned back inland we took a last look over the Blackwater towards Bradwell. The twin reactors were clearly visible on their peninsula, guardians of the river mouth. The careful grey of these colossal concrete chambers highlighted rather than concealed them, and they appeared to hover on the edge of reality like an industrial mirage. Their unstable connection to the physical realm matched that of the channels around them, constantly flooding inland to realign the coastal map before melting away. The plant relied on huge volumes of water drawn from the mouth of the Blackwater to cool its reactor core. High technology working in sequential rhythm with the tides.

We turned inland, taking the line of the vanished railway.

Back in Tollesbury we were disorientated by our sudden transition from the vast Blackwater spaces to a village of apparent normality. Where land and sea met, the sky was an active participant rather than a backdrop to the landscape, but now it withdrew behind the familiar horizons of houses and pubs, gathered around one another for protection against the impossible spaces beyond.

VI

TENDRING

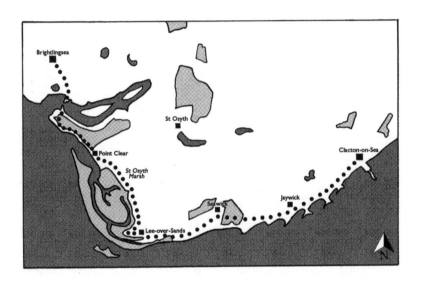

IT HAD NOT SEEMED WORTH staying up all night to watch the votes trickle in. So, when we woke to the EU referendum result we both felt numb. Live on radio the next morning, David Cameron resigned as Prime Minister, leaving an impossible problem of his own creation for someone – anyone but him – to sort out. When something out of the ordinary happens, it is felt as well as heard. Everyone could remember the few times national events have had a personal impact – usually a disaster, an act of terrorism, or something that hit too close to home. The vote to leave the EU crossed into a category beyond everyday government and political discourse, and the shock was visible on the faces of those who had made it happen, as well as those who had failed to see it coming, and had not understood what they had created. The pretence of a mainstream, consensus politics had been spectacularly overturned, and the guiding assumptions in place for a generation were up for grabs. For me, the Leave vote was a futile and self-destructive gesture, an exercise in flag-waving while drowning. Suddenly the future appeared much bleaker.

Before 1965, when London County became Greater London, Essex began at the Royal Docks. London had the Borough of West Ham, from Stratford to Woolwich, while Barking, Dagenham, Romford and Walthamstow were all in Essex. The new London consumed county towns in its hunger for land for larger basins, bigger factories and more space to house its workers. But today, the old county was reborn in the EU referendum, its shape revealed again on the voting maps. London was coloured yellow, for Remain, part of an island in the south-east surrounded by blue, for Leave. But the London Boroughs of Barking and Dagenham and Havering had voted Leave by large majorities, reaffirming their cultural allegiance to the east. Blue had eaten into the edges of Greater London, and the colour separation marked out a ghost impression of old Essex.

Britain is the most unbalanced country in Europe. Its people, wealth and productivity are located predominantly in London, which grows apace while the rest of the country lags. The dividing line is sharpest to the east of the capital, where the metropolis trails into the Essex towns and suburbs, lauded and mocked in equal measure. Through its keystone constituency of Basildon, Essex represented the Thatcherite revolution and the defection of working class voters to the Conservative party in 1979. Essex bought into the concept that, set free to fend for themselves, everyone would get what they deserved. It was an inspired angle; nobody thinks they are undeserving, but most are willing to give houseroom to the idea that their neighbours might deserve less. It was a philosophy that gave prejudice tacit permission to thrive.

Not long after the vote, we were waiting again at Liverpool Street Station, setting out to continue our walk along the Tendring peninsula, the slab of land that formed the easternmost part of Essex. It was a warm June night. Bishopsgate was packed. Groups of men stood outside in white shirts, jackets off. The Wetherspoons pub, a Victorian railway hotel dining room with the addition of fruit machines, had installed bag-searching bouncers with attitude. London seemed unsettled, and there was a tangible sense of uncertainty. Politics could not be as easily ignored as usual and no one was sure when, or whether, normality would return. It seemed an ideal time to get out to the coast, but we were less sure whether Essex was the place to get away from it all any more.

We took the Norwich train, with young, prosperous couples lining up pre-mixed G&Ts on their way to north Norfolk summer parties. At Colchester, we climbed the hill to find our stopover, an unlikely vegan B&B. The town was handsome in an Essex manner with wide market streets, fine, red-brick, Georgian town houses, a scattering of timbers. Its history was intimidating but caveated: the oldest recorded town in the country, Cymbeline buried in the local park. The city gates had been relocated within a system of underpasses, and the town entrance was guarded by a 1970s cement memorial to local physician and physicist William Gilberd. He was a Colchester man and Elizabeth I's personal doctor, but was also responsible for discovering that the core of the Earth was made of iron and that the planet was therefore magnetised. His experiments with the lodestone had provided an explanation for a phenomenon thought to be caused by magic, and reorientated subsequent journeys to magnetic north.

Colchester was also well-supplied with strip bars, top-shelf corner shops, army surplus warehouses, tattoo parlours. The pubs, however, seemed to have been made-over and, rather than the army drinking barns we had been led to expect, were enthusiastically selling craft beer. That morning police had been scrambled across the town centre after reports that the suspects in a kidnapping attempt at RAF Marham in Norfolk had been sighted near Colchester's army base. RAF Marham was a base for Tornados which were bombing raids over Syria. Two men 'of Middle Eastern appearance', one wielding a knife, had apparently tried to drag a soldier from his car, and the local paper, *The Daily Gazette*, had described the fugitives as the most wanted men in Britain. The excitement soon died down and several months later the police acknowledged that the incident was unrelated to terrorism.

The bus to Brightlingsea left late, after the driver had reached agreement with the powerful figure of the County Controller, without whose permission no bus left town. The route took us through the University of Essex campus, where novelist Lars Iyer had depicted a post-'68 generation of philosophy students who had tried to 'politicise their despair' by reconnecting to an Old European intellectual heritage. Since its days as a hotbed of student protest, the university had repositioned. The campus attempted to distract from its three brutalist towers with new blocks faced in red, orange, yellow, green and blue, architecture that was keen to be liked.

Research has shown that the Colne Estuary was treacherous, probably impassable. While the OS map showed a footpath that crossed Alresford Creek, online walkers reported a wade across the mud not to be attempted without the right equipment. Jules Pretty noted, 'The map says there is a ford over Alresford Creek. Not a chance.' There had once been a railway swing bridge but the line it served was closed and the bridge demolished. Brightlingsea has a Station Road and a Railway Hotel, but nothing to back them up since the Crab and Winkle Line from Wivenhoe to Brightlingsea had shut in 1964. The nickname was contested, used by two other redundant lines – one in Kent, and the other just across the River Colne at Tollesbury – but the common factor among all three was a complete lack of trains.

Wivenhoe is best known for its oysters, a reputation

which dates back to the Romans and beyond. Norden wrote that 'Essex yealdeth the best oysters in England'. Defoe wrote, 'On this shoar also are taken the best and nicest, tho not the largest oysters in England ... the chief place where the said oysters are now had, is from Wyvenhoo and the shoars adjacent.' They were then placed in barrels and taken upstream to Colchester, where they were sold as Colchester oysters. Defoe also reported that this coast was also known for its sole ('sometimes exceeding large'), turbot ('sometimes midling'), whiting, cod and flounder.

By the time the line fell victim to the Beeching cuts, it had already taken a considerable battering. When it opened in 1886 it connected the oyster beds of Brightlingsea to the railway network, but getting there involved constructing a railway to run along the coast beside the sea defences, crossing the mudflats in parts, and numerous creeks. It was an engineering feat, but the line was one of the most vulnerable in the country. The Black Monday floods of 1897, the worst North Sea storm of modern times until the 1953 Great Flood, submerged the entire line and stranded a train, whose passengers had to be rescued by boat.

The painter Francis Bacon lived and worked in Wivenhoe during the 1950s. He stayed in an 18th-century cottage on Wivenhoe Quay that was owned by his friends and fellow hell-raisers, Denis Wirth-Miller and Richard 'Dicky' Chopping. Chopping designed the covers for Ian Fleming's James Bond books – skulls, roses, revolvers and playing cards – a much more home-made aesthetic than was later applied to the films. Wirth-Miller, a painter, also helped 'Wivenhoe's Alfred Wallis', the primitivist Ernie Turner who became a great success when he retired as a shipwright to paint full-time. Bacon, Chopping, Wirth-Miller and friends drank together in the local restaurants and pubs, developing a reputation for what the *Ipswich Star* described in 2016 as 'week-long parties of hedonistic excess', leading proprietors to hide the champagne when they showed up. Wirth-Miller's paintings are dominated by Essex skies, trees and water, gently bleeding hallucinogenic hues. Although Bacon painted in the Wivenhoe cottage, surrounded by the drift of debris that always filled his studio spaces, he was an exclusively indoor painter and his work showed no apparent influence from the location.

Instead, we took the bus to Brightlingsea, where a foot-ferry crosses Brightlingsea Creek to the marshes beyond. Brightlingsea is still a port, but such a discreet one that we had to ask for confirmation. Discretion was the motivation when, during the 1984–85 Miners' Strike, importers began bringing coke into smaller, non-unionised ports from the Netherlands to avoid pickets. These included Wivenhoe and Brightlingsea, where flying pickets from Durham (perhaps descendants of those who left the Dengie in the 19th century) and South Wales clashed with police while attempting to prevent ships from unloading.

Brightlingsea was back in the news for similar reasons in 1995, when the livestock industry attempted to open a new route for live animal exports to the continent. Abattoir closures in Britain had caused cattle and sheep to be transported on ferries, in grim conditions, for slaughter in Europe. When public opinion caused ferry companies to back out, exporters sought less visible alternatives. The Battle of Brightlingsea lasted for most of the year

as protestors, mostly local women, prevented ships from loading while riot police piled in. The lorries carried sheep, but also cattle and veal calves, and it was the latter which became symbolic of the affair. The stand-offs ended when the exporters cut their losses, and soon afterwards the saga was forgotten amid the spread of bovine spongiform encephalopathy – or 'mad cow disease' – in Britain. More than 20 years later, the Brexit vote had revived calls to ban live animal exports as part of a changed relationship with the EU.

We walked through the small town to the port, which we could not see, obscured as it was by a large riverfront development which looked like every other marina on the south coast. The jetty carried 'No crabbing beyond this point' signs. Brightlingsea Creek lay broad, grey and mirror-still. Low islands of salt marsh appeared as strips of green and brown between the water and the horizon, weighted down under a heavy dome of sky. To the east, Cindery Island was practically invisible, but the map showed it to be pocked with disused oyster pits. The tidal channel around its far side is called The Folly, presumably an indication of how navigable it is, and leads to a miniscule blob of land among the mud of St Osyth Creek, named Pincushion Island.

The ferry to Point Clear was a two-minute journey in a tiny craft operated by two friendly lads. Their crossing technique involved sailing straight at the Point Clear shingle beach like a landing craft and dropping the prow to let us off. The ferrymen told us that when the port at Brightlingsea had gone into decline and the big ships had stopped coming, churning the river bed with their screws, the deep-water channel had silted up. It was now being dredged, and they hoped it would bring back lost business. In the meantime, they recommended a visit to the Stone Point Martello Tower nearby, but warned us against venturing further south, claiming, "It's all darkness out there." They were referring,

I assumed, to Clacton-on-Sea, regarded locally as a blot on the landscape because of the seaside poverty with which it has become associated. It has not always been this way. In 1939, *Highways and Byways in Essex* claimed, 'Clacton is to Southend as a moule marinière is to a winkle.'

Point Clear comprised the Martello Tower and a tiny café that served an eclectic menu including kebabs, teacakes and 'becon'. The Tower was accompanied by a battery commanding Brightlingsea Reach and the mouth of the Colne. It is the first in a set of 11, labelled 'A' to 'K', ranged along the Tendring peninsula from Point Clear to The Naze. They were built in the early 1810s as a defence against Napoleonic invasion. A small naval reserve station remained here until the mid-19th century. An observation post from the Second World War also survived. The rifle range is now occupied by the Orchards Holiday Park. The sea-wall took us past caravans and a chalet with tabloid press cuttings taped over its windows, all expounding conspiracy theories about the European Union. It was the type of house that seems to be hidden somewhere in every place, with an air of abandonment and a sense of an occupant who had long since parted company with reality. But this outlandish tabloid material was now embedded in mainstream political debate. What had once seemed absurd was now the stuff of nightmares.

From Point Clear, the status of the coastal footpath became uncertain. The map showed a break in the sea-wall south of Point Clear, where marsh spread between Ray Creek and the potato fields of Lee Wick Farm. No footpath was marked, and a single online report suggested the coast route was impassable. We studied the map for clues and saw the Ordnance Survey colours bleaching to marsh blue, mud grey and white, the tiny arrows that marked the embankment tailing away in an alarming fashion. This section of coast was almost entirely unvisited, and we were unhappy at

the choice between wading across a creek and retracing miles of walking. Defeated by the practicalities of walking a route full of blank spaces, we diverted across the potatoes to cut off the corner and reach solid sea-wall again.

At last the coastal marshes opened out. The lipped concrete causeway snaked through tidal lagoons, with the wooded rim of Mersea Island to the west. Sails dotted the mouth of the Blackwater, white and rust-red. We were somewhere on the coast, standing on the hard boundary between land and sea, gazing

out along the Colne saltmarshes towards the North Sea and the Belgian coast.

On St Osyth Marshes first impressions suggested a landscape of nothing but marsh and sea-wall, but the emptiness resolved itself as the detail came into focus. Swallows lined up on turquoise electricity cables, luminous against a darkening sky. Trails of small Gatekeeper butterflies rose from the long saltmarsh grass around our feet. A flutter of sparrows, too many to count, settled and resettled on a chainlink fence. Out on the saltings clean, white, angular egrets spotted us hundreds of yards away and lifted up into the broad sky. Old oyster pits beyond the sea-wall were filled with sea purslane.

St Osyth, east of Point Clear, was named after a dissolved abbey and a forgotten saint. Osyth was the daughter of Frithewald, King of the East Saxons. A nun, she had intervened to protect her sisters from the raiding Danes and was beheaded for her trouble. She is said to have picked up her now separated head and to have left a bloody handprint on the church door to indicate where she wished to be buried. On the spot where she was executed, Nun's Wood in St Osyth Park, a spring is said to have risen from the ground.

Ten women from St Osyth were executed for witchcraft during the 16th and 17th centuries. The best-known case involved

Elizabeth Bennet and Ursula Kemp. They were hanged in Chelmsford after confessing to using black magic to murder their neighbours. Both seem to have been local healers and midwives who fell out with a family whose baby had died, and were accused of cursing the child. In the 1920s two skeletons were discovered in St Osyth and exhibited as the remains of the two women, with a charge for viewing them.

Before the 1930s there was almost no settlement between St Osyth. West of Tendring was marsh. This isolation made St Osyth, according to James Wentworth Day, a prime spot for drug smuggling. Writing in 1949, he alleged that the 'short sea traders', ships plying back and forth across the North Sea from the Low Countries, would regularly smuggle cigars, perfume, silk, watches, brandy and Dutch schnapps. He also claimed that a Dutch barge would drop drugs off Point Clear in tins weighted with rock salt, which would dissolve after a couple of days allowing the containers to rise to the surface for collection, 'and another den in the Christian city of London got its supply of heroin [sic] or cocaine.' Wentworth Day was an unreliable source and strangely obsessed with smuggling, but there was no doubting the particular isolation of Point Clear, projecting out into the North Sea like an Essex overbite.

During the second half of the 20th century, the marshes

acquired isolated settlements, temporary structures and peripheral habitation. Lee-over-Sands resembled a collection of polar huts and appeared to have been constructed with whatever lay to hand. It was presided over by a concrete box, elevated on four legs, its purpose not apparent. The sea-wall drew us across the saltings to Seawick, a static caravan park and some slightly more permanent buildings. The 1960s map shows a crossroads with a pub, St Osyth Marsh on all sides. Since then Seawick had arrived. It is perhaps the cheapest place to live in southern Britain, with caravans advertised at £160 a month.

We stopped for lunch at a single-storey, pre-fab café and members' club called the Village Inn Pub, set among bungalows. We admired a lusciously furred white husky dog behind a picnic table. Its owner sported a similarly luscious white moustache and home-inked tattoos. He complained that the dog had lost his nerve, getting spooked one night for no apparent reason, and had not been the same since. The dog hid under the table. "Maybe he'll get over it?" we suggested, but it had been 18 months and the owner was convinced it was too late.

Another Martello Tower marks the transition from Seawick to Jaywick. The most vulnerable part of England is the Kent coast, closest to France, but the complete chain of 103 Martello towers stretched all the way from Seaford in Sussex to Aldeburgh in Suffolk. The only towers in Essex were on this stretch of coast, although Harwich possessed a supersized version called The Redoubt. The towers had been out of military use since the Second World War but still looked menacing, ready in case things flared up again across the water.

Across the shingle, a line of chalets became visible. They seemed to have landed on the pebbles complete with fenced front gardens, served by unadopted roads and surrounded by scattered rubbish heaps piled with mattresses, waiting for a match. This was the 'plotlands' development at Jaywick Sands, an outsider community notorious as the poorest place in Britain. The Government's Index of Multiple Deprivation ranked it as the single most deprived council ward in England, worst off in a long list of categories including income, employment, education, health, crime and quality of living environment.

Jaywick is an anomaly, a former resort where holiday homes were built in the 1920s and 1930s for Londoners on empty sands west of Clacton-on-Sea. After the war the chalets became permanent as it supplied much-needed, but illegal, housing. While other plotlands developments were bulldozed, Jaywick survived; the settlement was badly hit by the 1953 Great Flood, in which 35 residents drowned. The water came at Jaywick from both sides, rushing over the sea-wall and around from the north, filling up the low ground where the houses stood. Hilda Grieve's account is chilling: 'The Jaywick saucer filled in some places in a matter of fifteen minutes or so, so fast that people died in their beds without moving.' The surge reached Jaywick early in the morning, having swept over all of coastal Essex to the north in the preceding hour. 'The clocks in the Jaywick bungalows, on mantelpieces, tables and walls, were stopped at two o'clock.' Aerial photographs of Seawick show nothing but water with caravans,

chalets and a double-decker bus floating. No land can be seen at all.

Jaywick has become, along with Canvey Island, symbolic of a flood which has never left the minds of those living behind the Essex sea-walls. Essex County Council imposed special planning restrictions on Jaywick, and a main sewage system was only installed in the 1990s. Streets remained unadopted, chalet-style houses in poor repair, some collapsing while still inhabited. The entire place hovers on the brink of shanty town status. Despite

repaired and improved coastal defences, the houses also remain highly vulnerable to a tidal surge.

Unemployment and drug and alcohol problems were played out in Channel 5's controversial documentary *Jaywick: Benefits by the Sea*, broadcast in 2015. But Jaywick is no seaside freakshow. As we passed through the town, the sea-wall was busy and many of the houses were decorated in curious seaside styles, one bungalow painted all over with shamrocks. An enormous seated Buddha occupied one end of a suspended, first-floor conservatory. A woman with a small dog was looking for another, which was elderly and had disappeared on a dementia wander.

On the beach, a group of boys took turns to throw stones at a warning sign from very close up indeed. On the horizon an array of wind turbines had become visible, off Clacton. They seemed to float just below the vanishing point, drawing down energy like Walter De Maria's *Lightning Field* sculpture in the New Mexico desert, a thicket of steel conductors begging to be set alight. This is the Gunfleet Sands windfarm, jointly owned by the Danish firm DONG Energy and the Japanese Marubeni Corporation. In a largely unheralded change to the seascape of Britain, around 25 offshore wind farms have been constructed since the turn of the century. Most are located off the east coast, from the far north of Scotland all the way to the Thames Estuary, and include the largest windfarm in the world, the London Array. Gunfleet Sands opened in 2010 and now consists of 50 turbines, like a reinforcement crossing the North Sea to join the machines that had made landfall on the Dengie.

Turbines have become an integral part of the coast, and the sea cannot be contemplated without registering them. The experience of looking out to sea, entirely unchanged in its familiarity since man first stood on a beach, has been fundamentally altered within a decade, all around Britain. They create the sensation of an invasion force, always in the back of the eye, keeping coast watchers in a constant state of tension. Yet, despite this the turbines do not seem entirely malign; they exude a sense of mystery too. Their scale, as the only objects in view, is impossible to gauge and they seem to exist outside the accepted parameters of geography and time. They also offer an optimistic vision of the future, as the Bradwell reactors had sixty years earlier.

Suddenly, the sand became fine and pale, and the beach busy. We entered the outskirts of Clacton-on-Sea, the final destination for this leg of our journey, and the unmistakable signs of the seaside resort began to appear. Behind the Martello Inn Toby Carvery, a line of coaches was parked up in heraldic livery: Swallow, The King's Ferry, the galloping horse logo of Marshall's. Next door, a 1980s housing estate had been built on the site of the demolished Clacton Butlin's. S.L. Bensusan, recorder of marshland voices, had lamented the arrival of the holiday trade half a century before, writing in 1938 that 'the whistle of a widgeon on the saltings has been replaced by the blare of a jazz band from dance hall or restaurant.' Butlin's had opened its Clacton camp shortly before, only the second in the country. The miniature railway at Clacton became very well known, featuring in the closing credits of TV show *Hi-De-Hi!* It closed in 1983.

As we approached the pier, Saturday was in full swing. An Afro-Caribbean beach party, a hundred yards long, seemed to me at first to be a church outing but was equipped with a sound system, industrial drinks coolers and serious barbecues. The pier was packed with chaotic ice-cream queues, the PA banging out *Spirit in the Sky*. Nearly every stall was offering giant fluffy emojis as prizes. The atmosphere seemed less relaxed than the holiday setting suggested. As we left the promenade, a racist epithet floated out of the summer crowd crossing the road. The voice was slightly raised, as though others were meant to hear. I recoiled, and scanned the people around to see who had shouted, but there was no sign and no one else seemed to have noticed. I felt as though I must have imagined it, but I knew I had not.

As we crossed Clacton town centre, we passed the constituency office of Douglas Carswell, the country's only UKIP

MP. Carswell defected from the Conservative party in 2014 and was re-elected for UKIP by an overwhelming majority. He later explained that he had jumped ship specifically to 'decontaminate the UKIP brand', enabling its views to compete with Remain-supporting Prime Minister, David Cameron, and to prepare the ground for the Leave campaign. This highly calculated political manoeuvre was a complete success, enabled by the enthusiastic support of the people of Clacton. Carswell's switch had deftly reincorporated the once-marginal view of the nationalist right into the Conservative fold. Carswell was the only MP ever elected to represent UKIP, and was likely to remain that way. But his work was already done.

Just a short walk away is Frinton-on-Sea, best known for not being Clacton. Frinton's carefully cultivated reputation as a place apart is summed up in the claim that there were no pubs in the town until the 20th century. A Wetherspoons finally opened in 2000. Frinton has been much-mocked for its apparent prissiness, but the town has never been opposed to drinking, only to the public. There have always been plenty of bars, but they are found in members-only golf clubs or resident-only hotel bars. Frinton's defining characteristic is exclusion. The town's unofficial symbol is a pair of white, picket-fence style level crossing gates. When the gates were threatened with removal, the Mayor of Frinton told the world what he thought: 'Paris has its Eiffel Tower, London has Tower Bridge and in Frinton we have the gates. All over the world people talk about them.' Nevertheless, they were removed in 2009 by Network Rail 'under cover of darkness' and replaced with the standard gates found in every other town. This incident only helped to confirm suspicions in Frinton that nothing was the same anymore. The Mayor added: 'The gates provide a little enclave, it keeps us away from the madhouse. We want to protect our little bit of England.'

The appeal of the coast lies in its marginality, and its capacity to create a fantasy world, where normal rules of living are suspended. It attracts an unlikely combination of outsiders and insiders, neither with anywhere else to go. In Frinton, the insiders have retreated to the edge in a final effort to summon up their version of England. The concrete sea-walls reflect back ripples of disquiet.

VII

MERSEA

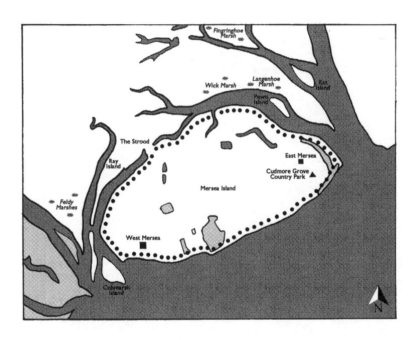

AFTER A GAP, during which we had found ourselves fully occupied with the demands of work, the late August Bank Holiday arrived. At home in south London everything was on hold as we waited for the Mastic Man, a demanding and mysterious figure who would perform a highly specialist task in our bathroom. His arrival might be unannounced; we were told he sometimes liked to surprise. Until he arrived, everything had to be "bone-dry", so the Essex expanses offered us humidity. We planned to walk around Mersea Island, before heading into the tangle of flats, estuaries and saltings between Tollesbury and Brightlingsea.

The third largest island in Essex after Canvey and Foulness, Mersea can be circumnavigated in a day. It is home to the nation's premier oyster beds and is itself shaped like an oyster, rounded and flattened into a hollow in the mainland, held between the estuaries of the Blackwater and the Colne. The coast around it is complicated, which was why we had not yet tackled the uncertain paths between Tollesbury and the River Colne. Landward of Mersea, the coastline was inaccessible on foot, blocked off by Abbots Hall Farm Nature Reserve and the Fingringhoe Firing Ranges.

Abbots Hall Farm belongs to the Essex Wildlife Trust, and is the site of what it calls 'coastal realignment'. The sea-wall was intentionally breached in two places in 2002, and the fields closest to the Salcott Channel have been returning to salt marsh ever since. The Wildlife Trusts and the Environment Agency are aiming to replace lost salt marsh, 60 per cent of which has vanished along the Essex coast over the past 20 years through the erosion caused by more frequent and violent storms. It is not just solid land that was being eroded, but also the buffer zones that were neither land nor sea. Realignment means that it is no longer possible to walk along this part of the sea-wall. Access further inland is restricted to weekday hours, and from a walker's point of

view this section of coast has ceased to exist.

To the north, the Fingringhoe Ranges occupy the tongues of land that flick, suggestively, towards Brightlingsea on the opposite bank of the Colne. These are Geedon Saltings, Fingringhoe Marsh, Langenhoe Marsh and Wick Marsh, but the sea-wall which snakes around them is inside a Danger Area cordon. The artist Mishka Henner has exhibited an aerial photograph, *D139 Fingringhoe*, taken from Google Earth. It forms part of a series of satellite images which show all that can be seen by the

public of the UK's many 'restricted zones'. The combination of empty land and proximity to London has made Essex vulnerable to invasion since the days of Byrhtnoth, and the remoteness is ideal for army training. Long stretches of coast have been requisitioned and militarised, barely noticed beyond the immediate vicinity.

Mersea Island is surrounded by a bewildering network of creeks and islets, and every scrap of land and sea has a name: Pyefleet Channel, Strood Channel, Mersea Fleet, Thorn Fleet, Besom Fleet, Brightlingsea Reach, Geedon Creek, Cobmarsh Island, Pewit Island, Rat Island, Ray Island. It is unclear which islands are tidal and which permanently separated from the mainland. Ordnance Survey maps surround the whole of Mersea with the wet, sand-brown colour that indicate mudflats.

To reach Mersea we travelled to Colchester. As we left the station, a full-sized billboard under the railway bridge proclaimed 'The Truth. Legal Name Fraud.' These posters had been appearing that summer all over England, a bizarre internet conspiracy theory about the ownership of an individual's identity which had spilled, unusually, into the physical world. In the same category as 'Flat Earth' conspiracies, it was a theory that defied all logic or evidence but thrived online because enough people believed that only they could see the truth, and that they were persecuted for their insight. Attempts to identify the funding behind the poster campaign had failed; the trail ended with a Canadian woman known as 'Kate of Gaia'. The appearance of these posters was, in retrospect, an omen of a summer in which fringe thinking had veered suddenly into the mainstream.

We found a heavily timbered, 15th-century coaching inn that did a good deal on bed and breakfast. Apart from us and the hotel staff, it appeared to be deserted, but the receptionist told us in a conversational tone that she was bothered by three ghosts: a basement monk, a boy in the breakfast room and Alice, a victim of thwarted love. A troop of ghost hunters had hired the place the night before, we were informed. One man had left early, upset by something he had seen. "You'd have thought he'd be happy," the receptionist commented. "That's what he came for." I recalled H.G. Wells wrote, 'Essex is so much more genuinely Old England than Surrey, say, or Kent.' The matter-of-fact acceptance of the past as part of the present, and of the supernatural as part of everyday life, was alien to us. Perhaps people here really saw things differently.

The bus to Mersea Island took a suburban route, tracing a slow loop around the suggestively named Lethe Grove, where the south Colchester estates were snared in enchanted oblivion. I was disheartened to see that the enormous pub that was the main feature of the village of Abberton was boarded up. The Great

Earthquake of 1884 had its epicentre near Abberton. Also known as the Colchester Earthquake, it was the strongest tremor in the British Isles since the 16th century, and damaged practically every building in Abberton and in Wivenhoe, as well as churches in the marsh villages. The church at Virley, to the south, was destroyed and only ruins now remain.

Out of sight of the village centre lay the expanse of Abberton Reservoir, used in 1943 by the RAF to practise bombing runs for Operation Chastise, the famous Dambusters' raid. The

reservoir, which had only opened in 1939, was the location for the final rehearsal for the attack on the Edersee Dam. It was simulated using flare guns, rather than the bouncing bombs that were used for real two nights later when the Edersee was breached, and 70 people killed in the consequent flooding. 'Danger! Troops Training' signs indicated the continued presence of the military, housed at Colchester Garrison and dispatched to train on woodland and marsh between the town and the sea. The Ministry of Defence, under pressure to dispose of its assets, had just announced the

sale of Middlewick Ranges on the southern fringes of the town between Colchester and Fingringhoe, to housing developers.

Mersea Island has a single access point, The Strood, a bridge across the tidal channel that separated it from the mainland. The road is submerged at high tide and cars obliged to wait it out on Mersea until the ebb tide arrives. The island is further from 'the mainland', as it is described, than it first appears. Red squirrels were reintroduced to Mersea Island in 2012, and are breeding successfully, appearing in back gardens. They were able to settle because Mersea had never had any greys, which were unable to tackle The Strood.

Successfully making the crossing on a single-decker, we paced out along a sea-wall which formed the most permanent feature of the shifting north shore. Signs warned of diversions and collapse, but the path was clearly visible retreating into the distance, the highest point in a flat, watery vista. The tall marsh grass had scorched to a dry yellow during the hottest East Anglian summer for a decade. We crossed a farm where the turf had been grazed short by sheep, cropped to the line of the causeway. The path seemed to pass along an illusory downland ridge above a valley flooded during a sudden coastal influx.

We turned the eastern corner of the island, opening up views across the Colne Estuary to the small harbour at

Brightlingsea. Among the trees a little way inland, we could make out a cement bunker among the trees, the last remaining trace of the East Mersea Starfish naval site, a Second World War decoy town. Staffed by film industry employees at Shepperton, the decoy programme was an elaborate exercise to confuse and misdirect German bombers. Highly convincing dummy airfields were built to draw fire by day, while at night bombed towns were simulated with lights, remote-controlled 'basket fires' and 'boiler troughs' creating the impression from the air of blazing buildings. The East Mersea Starfish was intended to protect the navy at Brightlingsea, on the opposite bank of the Colne, and there were two more in Essex, near Walton-on-the-Naze and Thorpe-le-Soken. At the Ford factory in Dagenham, in contrast, the roof had been painted to resemble marshland. The decoys were a success, attracting a substantial proportion of the bombs intended for real towns and cities. The coast proved ideal for conjuring illusions, temporarily anchoring places that would be gone when the tide turned and the sea mist lifted.

At Mersea Stone Point, the easternmost point of the island, we searched in vain for the remains of the lost Tudor fort, and were unable to detect anything resembling the stone. The fort site, we later discovered, was only apparent from the air. Mersea Fort was built during the reign of Henry VIII, as part of a chain of coastal forts and blockhouses. Henry's divorce of his first wife, Catherine of Aragon, angered Pope Paul III, who called for an invasion of England. It never happened, but the Device Forts, as they were known, ringed the south coast. As well as Mersea, forts were built at Osea, Brightlingsea and three at Harwich, all now lost. Mersea was refortified with each new European threat, including the Napoleonic Wars, but was now lost to the sea, its triangular plan visible only from the vantage of a satellite or drone.

Uninhabited East Mersea began to give way to well-visited beaches. A Scout camp on Essex County Council land had pitched heavy green canvas tents, the same model we both remembered from childhood camping trips in the 1980s. Great care had to be taken not to touch the sides in wet weather as it would break the seal, letting in the rain. At Cudmore Grove Country Park, where pre-historic elephant and hippopotamus bones have been found, the cliffs were low and crumbly. The coastal defences, built to fight an invasion that never came, have fallen as the friable, ochre soil has given way. The beach below was strewn with tumbled pill boxes and bunkers, concrete lozenges spilled towards the North Sea. Holidaymakers perched on fallen Second World War infrastructure, texting.

The coast here is retreating fast, trees falling in slow motion as the subsoil washes steadily away. To keep Mersea intact, polders have been laid offshore. These low fence lines mark out fields in the sea and were a Dutch invention to trap sediment and keep the sea back. The polders seemed to be struggling, but the dogs and bank holiday families were taking no notice. At Coopers Beach Holiday Park, static caravans were grouped around what 19th-century maps show to have been a duck decoy pond. The isolation and desertion of the Essex marshlands was evaporating, and the narrow road to Coopers Beach Holiday Park soon became congested with brand new white Land Rovers and the odd Porsche. For the first time on the Essex coast, we found ourselves following the money.

Our lunch stop was a small pub with a car park full of high-end transport, drawn by the seafood. Mersea's not-so-secret weapon is the native oysters fattened in its channels since before the arrival of the Romans. Mehalah's, a foodie stop in the middle of nowhere, was named after Mersea's one-and-only novel. It was written by the polymath parson at the nearby church, St Edmund the King, Sabine Baring-Gould.

It is said that four of the five bells of St Edmund's were stolen in the 16th century by robbers who attempted to remove them, naturally, by boat. The weight sent their vessel to the bottom, but the bells were recovered and later inspired one of the best-loved hymns of the 19th century. The ringing of the bells at his church is said to have given Rev Sabine Baring-Gould the tune for 'Now the Day is Over'. If Baring-Gould is now remembered, it is for his many hymns, but particularly for this and 'Onward Christian Soldiers'. However, he accomplished a great deal more, and still has his own appreciation society. A man of broad interests, he spent 10 years as rector of East Mersea during the 1870s and came, grudgingly, to admire the place. *Mehalah* opens with a tour-de-force description of the Blackwater and Colne tidal marshes. 'A more desolate region can scarcely be conceived,' he wrote, 'yet it is not without beauty.'

Baring-Gould was born in Devon and, after a career as a teacher when he would take classes with his pet bat perched on his shoulder, took holy orders. As a curate in West Yorkshire, he married the young daughter of local mill worker, Grace Taylor, an unconventional match. The couple were together for 48 years and had 15 children. Baring-Gould was a pioneering collector of folk songs and a prolific author who published at least 150 works, most of which he wrote standing up. These included a 16-volume *Lives of the Saints*, books of West Country characters and 'strange happenings', ghost stories, tales of werewolves and *The Curious Myths of the Middle Ages*, a favourite of H.P. Lovecraft. His writing, which also included many novels, ranged across Europe from Iceland to the Languedoc, from the wild Cornish coast to the salt mines of Cheshire.

His Essex masterwork, *Mehalah: A Story of the Salt Marshes*, was a sensation, a dark, elemental, family tragedy compared favourably by contemporaries to *Wuthering Heights*. It was very popular locally, and Ronald Blythe claimed that 'many girls were named after its heroine.' The novel is a dramatic and dark book in which the landscape is the dominant character. It opens on the tiny Ray Island, where an old woman shivering with fever insists that she caught it on Mersea – the mainland – and that there is no ague on 'The Ray'. The rather misogynistic plot involves the heroine, Mehalah Sharland, beset by the advances and violent persecution of her evil landlord, Elijah Rebow. At its hope-free ending, the bells of St Edmund's peal across the empty sea.

Mehalah does not cast Mersea in a pleasant light. While Baring-Gould appreciated the landscape, he was not so complimentary about the people. He wrote, 'The Essex peasants were dull, shy, reserved and suspicious ... I never managed to understand them or they to understand me ... As far as I could see there were not many persons of value, as readers and thinkers, with whom to make friends.' He was taken aback by the poverty and the 'uncouthness' of the local children, who were poorly dressed, often in leftover, cut-down military uniforms. He complained that his own children's faces became sore from exposure to the biting east wind. He was heckled during the Christmas Day service by his own parish clerk, who was drunk.

In 1881 he was relieved to return to Devon, where he felt he belonged. Despite the impression he left on Mersea, the island occupied only 14 pages of his memoirs, crowded out by chapters with more exotic titles such as 'Bohemia', 'Rome Revisited' and 'Les Eyzies'. However, he told a farmer's wife who longed to see Switzerland, 'I have seen the snowy Alps from the Schänzli above

Berne; but I have seen more splendid landscapes here.'

Back on the south shore, we found the coast path fenced and diverted. Climbing over we discovered a stretch of concrete-topped sea-wall that had been broken into sections and tossed like dominoes by the crumbling cliff. The coast seemed to be melting away before our eyes, and the horizon shimmered across a timeslip. At its far edge the island was being undermined by the sea and, while visitors sunbathed on the remains, I felt for the first time on our walk that this section of coast would not be here for

much longer.

Oyster shells had collected in vast quantities and formed a special Mersea version of a shingle beach. The shells crunched under our boots. A staple part of the common diet until the 19th century, when supplies began to dwindle, oysters were plentiful in the waters around Mersea. The island has been famed for its oyster production since very early times. The Romans, arriving in Essex to deal with the Iceni, had stayed to fortify Colchester and had laid oyster beds at Mersea, where they liked to come on holiday. Oyster farming rights on Mersea dated back to Edward the Confessor. Shellfish have now become the very fabric of the island.

The rights to the oysters of the Colne Estuary and the Mersea channels are still claimed by Colchester. In a ceremony that dates to the 12th century, the Mayor of Colchester asserts the town's rights over the oyster fisheries at the start of each oyster-dredging season. In September, he makes a ceremonial visit by boat to the Pyefleet Channel to trawl for the first oyster, which is toasted with gin and gingerbread. Colchester lost control of Mersea oysters sometime in the mid-19th century, but clung to its coastal connection. The annual Oyster Feast is held in October. The 2016 instalment was to be sponsored by a triumvirate of housebuilders: Bloor Homes, Bellway and Taylor Wimpey.

Meanwhile, despite the upgraded status of the oyster, from cheap protein source to expensive delicacy, the island is surrounded by evidence of its past. The oyster shells of Mersea were piling up on the shore, displacing the shingle, and forming a protective bulwark around a fragile island.

The beach huts of West Mersea inched into view, lined up along a mile of sand in uncompromising pastels. The heat was suddenly intense, searing the bathers but pursued by a weather system that was stacking tall, dark clouds over the Blackwater Estuary. As we hit town, the sun had disappeared and a line seemed to be drawn under the long, dry summer. The narrow pavements of West Mersea were full and its pubs and oyster restaurants fully booked. Outsized Range Rovers were parked up outside, next to a wide, peculiar, tidal mudflat, where houseboats sat in empty, water-carved channels, linked to dry land by wobbly private causeways. The channel beyond is known as The Gut.

    The connection between Mersea and wider global events came as a surprise. Although the island seemed a long way from mainland concerns, it was clearly feeling the pressure. A poster protested against Colchester Borough Council's plans to build houses in empty East Mersea, and prophesied 'The Mersea way of life, gone for ever.' The East Anglian polemicist James

Wentworth Day had described the development of West Mersea between the wars with contempt – 'this little Tooting, this petty Putney' – and loathed builders 'who bought the farmland that had grown the golden wheat for centuries.' His reactions were a foretaste of the 1980s, when a newly prosperous commuter culture emerged and detached houses began to appear on the edge of the marshes, dividing Essex into old and new. The islands and coastal settlements can be inward-looking and conservative. But the localism of the Essex coast, as lauded by reactionary writers, contrasts with its sea-born connections to the continent and the world beyond. It is a place of contradictions where fixed ideas of national identity slip away under closer inspection, leaving only the place and the moment.

Wentworth Day's self-consciously antiquated language expressed his retreat into a world of 'sportsmen' and duck hunting, apocryphal pub stories and recollections of the good old days, when the Dutch raided the Thames or King Alfred fought the Danes. Wentworth Day was an objectionable figure, briefly a celebrity when he appeared on the 1950s television series, *Out of Step* and *People in Trouble*, hosted by Dan Farson, which explored social controversies of the time, from nudism to mixed marriage. As the resident reactionary, Wentworth Day's outrageously racist views were part of the entertainment, until he went too far and called for all homosexuals to be hanged. This proved too much even for 1958. A prolific author, his 1949 *Coastal Adventure* combines dyspeptic social commentary, on farming practices in particular, with tall tales and an endless amount of shooting. His imperious description of the island – 'Mersea men live by the sea and the land, by the plough and the net, the gun and the tiller' – summed up the complexity in an apparently insignificant piece of coast.

The town's medieval lanes and high hedges were festooned with union jacks. They turned out to be left over from an island-wide party the previous night. West Mersea yachtswoman Saskia Clark had just returned from the Rio Olympics with a gold medal. With her sailing partner Hannah Mills, she had won the Women's 470 event. The yachting prowess traditionally associated with Mersea and neighbouring Tollesbury was as strong as ever. Clark belonged to the West Mersea Yacht Club, founded in 1899. Its clubhouse, on Coast Road, flew the red ensign with the addition of the Essex symbol of three 'seaxes', the fearsome Saxon scimitars said to be the original arms of Erkenwyne, King of the East Saxons.

For a small island, Mersea boasts a lot of writers, more than just mavericks such as Baring-Gould. Female crime writers seem to have an affinity with Essex, and two of the three Queens of Crime, the writers who along with Agatha Christie made their names between the wars, were based on the Essex coast. Dorothy L. Sayers lived in Witham, Margery Allingham in Tolleshunt D'Arcy, near Maldon, from 1935. Allingham's domestic life was complicated; she was the hostess at the centre of a local social scene with house parties and cricket at the club, but her marriage to her philandering husband, Pip Youngman Carter, was often unhappy, and she suffered from depression, which saw her institutionalised.

Allingham had spent holidays on Mersea Island as a child, and at the age of 17 took part in 'table-turning' sessions when the Allinghams 'tried the glass'. They made contact with a deceased local called Joseph Pullen who told them, through the Ouija board, stories of the Ship Inn, a gang of rum smugglers known as 'The Preventatives', a woman ducked as a witch, the barmaid, a Spaniard who loved her, and a murder. Remarkably, Allingham turned this story, obtained over several nights, into her first novel, *Blackkerchief Dick*. The seances continued, and Allingham wrote a story on Mersea called *Hill of His Ancestors*, in which a man who thinks himself 'modern' and superior to the locals finds himself compelled to climb a hill where he is projected back into ancient history. He encounters spirits with names such as Ferdal of the Dark Hill and Abenden, Son of Tor who came to Allingham in a séance. She gave up the practice soon after, becoming scared after encountering a 'Pan spirit' called Lobot of Gleet.

Later books set in the vicinity include *The Sexton's Wife*, a ghost story set in Tollesbury, and *Mystery Mile*, an Edward Campion book set on a fictionalised Mersea Island (the endpapers included an island map). The villain in the latter dies a grim, Mersea death, stuck in the mud at low tide: 'Not a foot away from him, was a thick white line, irregular, more terrible, more relentless than the mud itself, the tide.'

Where the small town ended, we passed out of Mersea and back onto the marshes, which opened up again as we walked the final leg back to the Strood. Barely visible as a smudge on the level horizon was Ray Island, the setting for *Mehalah*, now owned by the National Trust, a sandy hill, topped with low trees, and inhabited solely by Soay sheep.

Our island circuit was complete. We crossed back to the mainland, a transition back to the material world via the Colchester bus. The journey from mud and oysters to familiar, solid surfaces allowed us to acclimatise gradually, and by the time we reached London, Mersea Island seemed an illusion, an effect of heat on water.

Before our Mersea expedition I had read about an oyster fisherman who had recently discovered planks near Ray Island, hidden in the mud. On closer inspection they were revealed as the remains of a Bronze Age track. Archaeologists suggested that they were part of a system stretching out over farmland, now submerged under the sea, and that the tracks were evidence of an early form of enclosure, as land was carved into fields and an economic elite emerged through control of the land. This ancient track was just a hint of the world that lay buried under the sea, the vanished territory of Doggerland.

If Britain has an identity it is bound up in its separation from the Continent as an island standing alone. Imagine, then, the North Sea replaced by solid ground, forming a land border with the Low Countries and France. Rather than a smoothed, eroded edge, East Anglia is the bridge between inner England and northern Europe, the British Isles an elaborate peninsula. The missing piece is Doggerland, inundated 6,500 years ago and only now being rediscovered. Before the glaciers melted and sea levels rose, a land mass had linked East Anglia to the European mainland, and the modern-day Netherlands, Denmark and north-west Germany. As well as rising sea levels, the melting of the ice was thought to have lessened the weight bearing down on the land, causing it to tilt east. The final separation of Britain and Europe may have been caused by a sudden landslide off the coast of Norway, followed by a disastrous tsunami.

In all probability, Doggerland was an area of saltmarshes

and mudflats, much like the remnant coastal marshes in both Essex and the Netherlands. The Thames and the Rhine were thought to have met in what was now the middle of the North Sea, flowing together into the English Channel which was then their combined estuary. A lost land beneath the sea had been discussed since the late 19th century, when trawlers had begun to bring artefacts to the surface in mid-ocean: the remains of plants, lumps of peat, animal bones and Neolithic flint arrow heads. But it was only in the 2010s that the extent of Doggerland was mapped and Dogger Bank, on a latitude with Yorkshire, revealed as the northern hills of a Greater East Anglia. In 2018 Vince Gaffney, an archaeologist surveying the seabed for inundated settlements, described Doggerland as 'terra incognita' and suggested, 'The area is so large that complete cultures could be out there.'

Doggerland was a real-life Ultima Thule, a mythical land of the north where the sun went when it set. The work of the Greek explorer Pytheas is lost but a later author, Polybius, reported that he had walked Britain on foot and discovered a region called Thule 'in which there was no longer any proper land nor sea nor air, but a sort of mixture of all three.' Ptolemy later located Thule in the North Sea beyond Shetland. It reminded me of J.A. Baker who, on his marsh vigils, had sensed a place beyond: 'Morning was hooded and sealed with deep grey cloud and mist. The mist cleared when the rain began. Many birds fled westward from the river, golden plover high among them. Their melancholy plover voices threaded down through the rain the sorrowing beauty of *ultima Thule.*'

VIII

MARSH

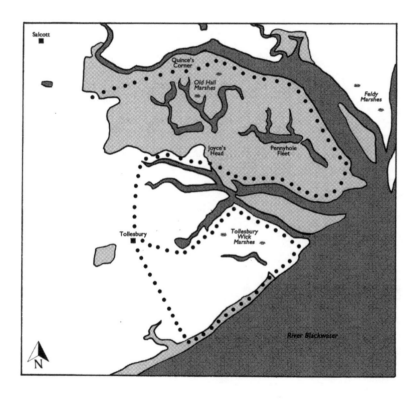

THE AUTUMN EQUINOX brought a collective groping towards normality after a summer of ominous political change. Jeremy Corbyn was re-elected as Labour leader that day with an increased majority, leaving 300,000 people feeling very optimistic. The rest seemed less sure, but there was no longer much room for nuance or perspective in British politics. The astonishing rise of the Labour party's most peripheral figure had been taken as a vindication by many who had probably expected their views to remain outside the mainstream all their lives. Now, they had been right all along, and if you were not with them, you were against them. This attitude had also become commonplace in pro-Brexit rhetoric. Terms closely associated with repression, such as 'traitors' and 'collusion', had begun to appear on the front pages of the right-wing tabloids, aimed at judges as well as campaigners.

Our usual route east was closed. Crossrail, recently and unenthusiastically renamed the Elizabeth Line, was being built over several years of weekends, extending the reach of the Tube network deeper into Essex. We took the Central Line to Newbury Park, an obscure station in Zone 4 where buses made their lengthy way to the usually well-connected towns of Essex. The station was dominated by a barrel-vaulted, concrete bus garage, an austere Festival of Britain statement of intent. The journey quickly became a Modernist field trip as we cruised past the beltway bungalows that lined the A12, traversing the bypass sprawl of Havering, Gallows Corner and Harold Wood. It was an uncertain zone that occupied few mental pictures of London. This is where London and Essex had become one between the wars through the ribbon development that connected towns such as Romford and Ilford to east London.

Colchester, familiar now after a summer of visits, was our starting point for a final time. On the western edge of the town Lexden Mound is said to be the burial place of Cymbeline, king of the lost eastern Celts. We had seen Shakespeare's play of the same name two days earlier at the Globe in London, where it had received an urban makeover. Cymbeline had become a North Face-clad drug dealer, while Belarius had retreated to the Welsh hills to grow skunk. It was billed as 'the London Cymbeline', but the accents were distinctly Essex, which is everyone's idea of London street speak – how to talk rough. It was both entertaining and entirely misguided. It soon turned out that it was also the final straw for the Globe's management, who ended Emma Rice's contract as Artistic Director not long after. While they liked the theory of shaking up their thatched theatre, the reality was a different proposition.

Meanwhile, in Cymbeline's real capital, the days had

suddenly become shorter and Saturday nights started sooner. The high street bars were packed, everyone dressed for ritual, intensive weekend enjoyment. An SOS Bus was parked up, offering water, ready to deal with the evening's fallout. It advertised emergency first aid, or somewhere to retreat if you were 'feeling threatened'. Colchester's few streets felt on edge. There were more people begging on the street than we could reasonably account for, and they were all very young.

Our B&B was timber-framed – standard for Colchester – and maze-like. Its bookshelves were stocked with Bruno Bettelheim, Arthur Koestler and Ayn Rand, less bed and breakfast and more 1970s Hampstead study. A fellow guest, a gentleman in his 60s with a trim, white moustache and linen suit, had just flown in from Thailand for his annual stay. The Snake Brand talc in the bathroom belonged, presumably, to him.

We were heading for some of the most isolated parts of the Essex marshes, the ephemeral acres of land east of Tollesbury. A taxi was the only transport available, but the driver complained that his company had been plagued by phantom call-outs to isolated spots on the marshes. When the car arrived, he explained, there was no passenger to be found. We drove across the Abberton Reservoir dam again, imagining the barrel bombs as they kissed the water and rushed spinning towards us. Abberton was a flooded valley – the valley of the Roman River – named after earlier occupants of its banks. The place-names by the water seemed to connect directly back to different historical eras: the village of Layer-de-la-Haye sounded distinctly Norman, and Blind Knights farm positively Arthurian.

We followed the sea-wall which tracked the outer limits of Old Hall Marshes, a lolling tongue of land. Its meandering edge was 10 miles around, and deserted. Jonathan Raban, approaching from the south in a yacht, struggled to identify the substance of

the place: 'The thin pale water didn't look like sea, and nor did the land around it look like land. It was wide-open, flat and boggy, only by a few degrees less liquid in its consistency than the stuff which was officially designated as water on the chart'. The moon-pulled marsh is ideal for avocets, the rare wading bird that is also the symbol of the RSPB. A substantial proportion of the UK population of avocets lived out there, but they must have been hiding from us.

The map named just two features on Old Hall Marshes,

Quince's Corner and Joyce's Head, and showed a couple of creeks. Otherwise, the map was blank. We walked the weaving causeway, raised above waterlogged channels and mud formations electric green with eelgrass. We encountered only a single figure, a trail runner who approached very gradually from the far horizon along the sea-wall path. When we eventually met, the three of us performed an awkward, silent dance on the narrow bank top, surrounded by cows and water.

The dome of the sky and the sharp, spirit-level skyline made it only possible to focus either on the vast, estuarine cloudscape or the tiny detail of the marsh grasses. On the saltings, the redshanks, 'sentinels of the marsh', squeaked like car alarms. Reed banks, rustling like dry paper in the breeze, provided the ambient soundtrack. The marshes had once been prime shooting country. James Wentworth Day had reminisced, in an alarming manner, that in the inter-war period on Old Hall Marshes '[i]t was no uncommon thing for five or six guns to kill two to three hundred duck on the opening morning of the 8th of August.'

When we reached Pennyhole Fleet, marked on the map in lake blue, there was no water. The lake bed was cracked, white mud. It seemed the driest spot in what is the driest county in Britain. An 'absolute drought' had been declared across southern England that summer, and the winter to come would be the driest in two decades. It seemed impossible in such as watery place, but out on the marshes the evidence was clear.

The novelist John Fowles was born in Leigh-on-Sea and wrote the introduction to the 1969 edition of *Mehalah*, in which he described this area: 'The Essex marshlands that stand north from Shoebury Ness to Clacton form still a strange *terra incognita*.' He continued, in misanthropic tones, 'It is not English, though it lies so close to the termite heart of England; but spiteful, anti-human, a Beckett nightmare waiting for the world to grow desolate again.' Fowles seems to have identified something essential about Essex, which was becoming apparent to us out here on the marshes: that it was an ideal place for retreat. The openness of the landscape left nowhere to hide, so generations had constructed their own palisades, but the purpose of retreat could be either to change or to remain the same. The novel which made Fowles famous, *The French Lieutenant's Woman*, ends with the sentence, 'And out again into the unplumb'd, salt, estranging sea'. Despite relocation to the West Country, the North Sea was still lodged in his consciousness.

We arrived at Tollesbury, which was shut under a soft grey lid, perceptions eroded by the sensory deprivation of Old Hall Marshes. The landlord of the pub in the centre of Tollesbury assured us, from behind a huge platter of cheese, that there was no food. We left for the marina, where all the activity in the village was focused on The Hard, the former fishing quay perched on the edge of Tollesbury Wick Marshes. A retired lightship, bright red, was moored offshore in Woodrolfe Creek where small boats lurked in muddy channels, waiting for the tide to float them free. This had been a fishing port, specialising in clams and oysters, with a fleet of expert boatmen. The reputation of Tollesbury's sailors was high, and they were sought after for skills honed in the teeth of the harsh east winds, steering through the shifting

mudflats. Wentworth Day described Tollesbury as 'that forgotten Essex marshland village that breeds the finest yachtsmen in the world.' Exposed to the North Sea, with nothing to stand in the way of the prevailing, offshore winds, Tollesbury men were ready for anything.

The 1930s were the glory days for Essex sailing, and for Tollesbury in particular, when sailors from the Blackwater and the Colne crewed Britain's yachts in the America's Cup. The Cup was always a rich man's pursuit, and the link with Tollesbury developed

from Edwardian sailing days. Fishermen from the village, and from nearby places including West Mersea and Wivenhoe, would work on oyster smacks and sail Thames barges during the winter, and in summer they would crew the yachts of the wealthy. In this capacity, they raced around Britain and across the Atlantic. The entire crew of six on the 1930 challenger, Shamrock V, came from Tollesbury. The village also featured on the 1934 and 1937 British challengers. In 1937, the yacht Endeavour went missing for 14 days after losing its tow rope, and crossed the Atlantic on its own, received with relief and a Pathé news crew on arrival in Gosport.

Our approach to The Hard took us past a curious set of wooden structures. The Yacht Stores were built in the early 1900s to house the sails for J-Class yachts, the type used in the America's Cup between the wars. Their Bermuda rigs formed a satisfying pair of triangles, a child's drawing of a sailing boat. The listed Stores were unique to Tollesbury and sat above ground level on squat stone pillars to keep their contents safe from the water.

Beyond The Hard, the marshes opened up again and all other human presence evaporated. We were soon the only two people in a landscape that stretched out far ahead, but the place radiated an almost overwhelming sense of presence. The autumn hedges were in full fruit, and the Tollesbury Marshes were loaded with an impossible crop of blackberries, haws and rosehips. The sloes were gone though, just a single fruit clinging on here and there. The red hills of the marshes, used to pan salt since the Bronze Age, could be discerned as low mounds prominent on the flat land, filled with charcoal, ash and clay.

In 1938, Wentworth Day claimed to have seen an unmarked black aeroplane landing on an unnamed marsh 'within ten miles of Colchester and within six miles of Maldon ... a peninsular between two creeks where the tide ebbs and flows and the coastguard seldom goes.' The unlikely scene mirrored H.G. Wells' vision of invading Martian machines. He muttered darkly about the threats he received when he wrote about what he had seen and speculated at length about the scale of smuggling into Britain via the east coast, which he believed to be commonplace.

A ship with black sails, the sun behind it, slipped silently into the Blackwater. Then we rounded the corner, turning back inland with the coast. A strong south wind came at us off the estuary, an auster, as the Romans called it, threatening sea mists. But the sun still shone at late summer strength, reflecting off the water of the dyke to reveal a glittering path west like a shining ley line, a track of light across eastern Essex. We sprawled on our backs on the roof of the concrete pillbox guarding Shinglehead Point. In his poem 'Journey Out of Essex', Michael Longley described the flight of the poet John Clare from his Essex asylum: 'I am lying with my head / Over the edge of the world, / Unpicking my whereabouts.'

We gazed at the unexpected view back to the west along the silver Blackwater. Charles Williams, a poet and friend of C.S Lewis with whom he had been described as a 'Christian fantasist', saw visions in the marshes. He wrote, 'My house is in the plains beyond the mouth of Thames / And built by the rushing wind and the tongued flames / Where the coast of Heaven borders the Essex coast, / And the byres of Essex are the shires of the Holy Ghost.'

The west is associated with death – the death of the sun – but also with transition into other realms beyond the horizon. The east is the land of the rising sun, of the new in all its forms, both welcome and threatening. Here, the two were equal, a balancing point in the landscape.

The marshes were capable of being both enchanting and fetid, depending on mood. Jonathan Raban, far from enchanted with the empty country, wrote, '[t]hese charmless and forbidding marshes had been the making of London as a world city.' He

pointed out that the flat land to the east of London allowed shipping to reach the city with the wind behind it all the way, unimpeded by hills. Meanwhile, London itself remained 'England's snuggest port ... protected from the sea by a boggy plain of what looked and smelled like its own excrement.' His cynical analysis typifies the stereotype of Essex as a land laid to waste by the greedy demands of the capital, a dumping ground where everything of value had been spoiled. This story dogs the county, but now I was beginning to understand the glorious landscapes it concealed. I began to wonder why anyone would want to change it.

We had talked the spooked cab company into coming back to collect us from the Tollesbury bus shelter, where we had ended our last, hay-fever-ridden visit. The driver was ex-army and had stayed on in Colchester when his posting ended to marry a local girl like, he said, many others. From Colchester Station it was a long journey on bus and train to Newbury Park, but the marshes had been necessary and fortifying. We would not be returning to Colchester in the foreseeable future. We were done with the Blackwater, the Colne and Mersea. Our next visit would see us in fresh territory, working past Walton-on-the-Naze to different marshes, this time on the Stour.

IX

THE NAZE

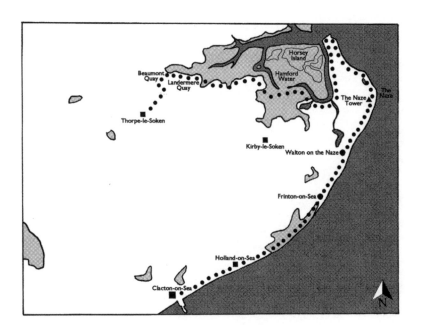

SINCE OUR WALK HAD BEGUN in the spring of 2016, the West had been busy dismantling itself. The election of Donald Trump as US President in November 2016 turned what we still forlornly hoped was a social blip into a full-scale culture shift. Perhaps this was what it felt like to get older, but this was someone else's reality. When B-movie star Ronald Reagan was elected as the actual President, that too must have made people feel dizzy. This time, the parallel storylines of reality TV, which had been central to the experience of the 21st century so far, had switched seamlessly into the real world. The irony of reality TV is that it is anything but real. If you do not like the storyline, you invent your own. If the story is that politics is a corrupt elite, an outsider is the only person to break the cycle. If the outsider is a ludicrous, impulsive, childlike egotist, so much the better – politicians are controlled and measured, so here is proof that Trump is not one of them. It was all darkly and inevitably logical. The empty vessel at the head of the Western world, with no reason to cultivate trust, principles or public good, was a terrifying figure.

In Britain, a political storm that had been gathering around the eastern fringes was now lashing the whole country. We returned to Essex on 2nd October 2016, the day Article 50 was triggered. In the few months since the referendum, the daily news had been dominated by intensely technical arguments. An arcane treaty clause had suddenly become crucial, but there was no consensus on what it meant when put into practice. Article 50 of the Treaty of European Union simply states: 'A Member State which decides to withdraw shall notify the European Council of its intent.' This simplicity masked a maze of implications; after all, the clause had been drafted on the assumption that it would never be used. This version of the future had not been part of the plan.

Meanwhile, 'Brexit' had become commonplace. The word was used so often its absurdity was forgotten within days. The EU referendum had created a new language, enormous implications packed into a portmanteau word, or hidden behind a paragraph number.

The Friday night train from Liverpool Street had shed all its other passengers by the time it reached Walton-on-the-Naze, the end of the line. It was still out of season; Walton was deserted. The car showroom lighting the seafront turned out, on closer inspection, to be a large mobility scooter dealership. In the luminous bay window of a seaside block a woman stood motionless, back turned, wearing an old-fashioned hat and coat, as though she had spent 30 years ready, waiting for someone. The pub where we had booked a room contained only a barman, whose elaborate jollity – "Greetings, good Sir" – failed to fill the empty saloon. On the first floor, we opened a door to find a full-sized ballroom, with gilt decoration, hinting at a Victorian resort past that had long-since faded out.

From the beer garden we saw two lights far out in the blackness, beyond the pier, flashing in sequence with each other. Their message was undecipherable, but next morning we calculated that they belonged to the Sunk Light Vessel, far out in the North Sea, and to the independent territory of Sealand. A deserted Second World War anti-aircraft platform called Rough Sands or Roughs Tower, Sealand had become famous after declaring independence in 1967. The fort, eight miles off the Essex coast, had proclaimed itself a sovereign territory following a strange series of violent confrontations at the height of the pirate radio boom.

Roughs Tower was one of four Maunsell Forts, freestanding platforms on two concrete pillars built to defend the Thames Estuary from German attack. A second type of Maunsell Fort, three sets of seven metal towers on spindly legs, were closer to Kent and look even more like special effects from early Doctor Who. They were the last in a series of Essex coastal defences that stretched back to the Device Forts of Henry VIII. Located just outside UK territorial waters and therefore beyond the jurisdiction of UK law, the Maunsell Forts later proved irresistible to pirate radio operators.

I have been fascinated by the story of Sealand for years, and it was a strange sensation to see such an unlikely place in the flesh, even as a tiny shape on the horizon. In 1967, an ex-army major called Roy Bates took control of the platform from pirate broadcasters who were already in residence. It is not clear how he achieved this, but he planned to install his own station – Radio Essex – which had previously broadcast from Knock John Tower, which was just inside British territory and therefore vulnerable to the authorities.

Ex-military and pirate radio proved a volatile combination. According to reports, men from Radio Caroline then tried to take over Fort Roughs from Bates and his son, Michael, but were held off. The Bates family was armed with petrol bombs. This was not the only violent incident involving competing pirate radio stations. A trial then followed in which Major Oliver Smedley, of Radio Caroline, was acquitted of killing Radio City's Reginald Calvert, shot in a dispute over transmitter equipment. Smedley successfully argued that he had killed Calvert in self-defence. An ex-solider with a Military Cross won during the Normandy campaign, Smedley belonged firmly in the category of political mavericks who floated around the Essex coast. He was a Gladstonian Liberal who campaigned for traditional Liberalism in the form of free trade, leaving the party in 1962 to found the 'Keep Britain Out' campaign, which opposed membership of the European Economic Community. He also ran a nightclub in Albufeira, Portugal.

After the Smedley trial, the government decided that pirate radio had gone too far and sent the Royal Navy to demolish the forts, even though they were technically outside British jurisdiction. They blew up Sunk Head Fort, but when they approached Roughs Tower, Bates and his son fired warning shots. Bates then declared independence from Britain. A court subsequently found that there was no case to answer, as the incident had happened outside the United Kingdom.

Bates took to his tiny country with enthusiasm, inventing a flag, passport and currency and declaring himself Prince Roy and his wife Princess Joan. In another outbreak of armed violence, a sub-Bond raid by a group of Dutch and German chancers led to the German government having to formally negotiate the release of one of their nationals, held for 'treason' by Bates because he carried a Sealand passport. Since then, governments had sensibly ignored the platform. Roy's son Michael inherited the title of Prince on the death of his father and devoted himself to flogging aristocratic titles and an impressive range of tourist bric-a-brac from the Sealand website. The story is murky and tacky in equal measure, but it is also compelling. The idea of an independent micro-nation just off the coast seemed too good to be true, a version of *Passport to Pimlico* come to life. It is begging to be filmed.

By morning, Walton had woken from its deep slumber. Our pub turned out to be a Georgian hotel and the elegant ballroom seemed slightly less unlikely in the daylight. The population of Walton includes both a retired contingent, and an alternative one,

with a higher proportion of blue dyed beards than any other part of the Essex coast so far. Sealand was still visible on the horizon, now revealed as a steel and concrete platform far out to sea, but there was no prospect of reaching it. Instead, we marched out of Walton to the north. The coast path led through a village of beach huts inhabited by friendly pensioners and out onto the Naze, home to the curious, octagonal Naze Tower.

The Naze is a corruption of the Old English word 'ness', meaning a headland. It protrudes into the North Sea in the general

direction of the Hook of Holland and is the easternmost point in Essex. Daniel Defoe, on his Essex tour, wrote, 'Here one sees a sea open as an ocean, without any opposite shore, tho' it be no more than the mouth of the Thames.' New paths have been recently cut through the gorse and the low trees, away from the collapsing cliff edge. The Naze Tower, built in 1720 as a warning beacon for shipping, is remarkably tall for its time. Its origins are not entirely clear; an earlier tower appeared on the same site in a map of 1594. It looked to me like a remnant of a vast, outlandish Tudor palace that had fallen into the sea.

Suffolk was visible from the top of the tower, up many spiral stairs, and Orford Ness lay flat along the horizon to the north. The rate of erosion beyond Orford, which famously drowned the medieval town of Dunwich, is matched only by the retreating cliffs on the Naze. The Naze had once extended more than four miles further out, but the original town of Walton was also under the sea. In 1789, as the French Revolution across the water shook the Continent, All Saints church had toppled off the cliff. The Naze has lost more land to the sea than anywhere in Essex and is now a delicate, wafer-thin promontory.

The whole of East Anglia is tilting. The geological shift that sank Doggerland continues; while the west coast rises the east is falling. The level of the land is around 13 feet lower than it was when the Romans arrived. The combination of falling land, rising seas and erosion make the soft Tendring cliffs particularly vulnerable. The Naze is losing two metres every year, but a new stretch of coastal protection has just been completed, designed to keep the Tower safe for another 100 years. In the gift shop we heard that the locals built their own defences on the Naze the previous summer, filling wire gabions with stones by hand to protect the town's sewage works. We were offered sharks' teeth, smooth and dark like flint, sold in small plastic bags. They were 20 million years old, collected in jarfuls from the beach. The erosion is releasing more of the past every day, and the local museum was full of auroch bones and mammoth teeth disgorged from the pre-Ice Age tundra.

The gantry cranes at the Port of Felixstowe, the largest in Britain, were visible through haze on the far side of the Stour Estuary. We turned the headland on fresh paths through the scrub, cut to replace last summer's tracks, which had already fallen into the sea. The Naze shelters a maze of small tidal islands, known officially as Hamford Water but dubbed in local parlance 'The Backwaters'. This is a place with competing fictional identities. It was 'The Great Marsh' in Paul Gallico's Dunkirk fable, *The Snow Goose*. He described it as 'one of the last wild places of England, a low, far-reaching expanse of grass and reeds and half-submerged meadowlands ending in the great saltings and mud flats and tidal pools near the restless sea.' It was also the setting of Arthur Ransome's 1939 book *Secret Water*, the eighth in his Swallows and Amazons series. The plot is based around a family holiday, interrupted when the Swallows' father is called back to his job with the navy, leaving the children to explore Hamford Water on their own. They pitch camp above the mud line, and sail the channels with their Amazon friends and newly arrived locals, the Eels, to map the hidden islands and saltings.

In theory, I knew this landscape in great detail, having pored over the book and the maps drawn by the children when I was young. However, unlike the Lake District settings of earlier Swallows and Amazons books, which I had visited on family holidays, I had no sense of the setting as a real place. As the islands of Hamford Water appeared in front of us, I now experienced the uncanny sense of an imagined world coming to life, gently unfurling with the tidal wash. *Secret Water* seemed a more complicated story than I had appreciated when I first read it. The sudden disappearance of the children's father, called away by his navy duties clearly presages the Second World War, which broke out as the book was published. His work took him to the naval training base at Shotley, only five miles to the north but out of sight beyond Harwich. In his absence, the older children trained for pre-determined roles in life: Susan practised the organisational skills she would need as a housewife; her brother John commanded a ship and charted unknown territory, which would serve him well in the colonies. Neither of the positions they prepared for would survive the war intact, and I wondered how the Swallows might have dealt with the social change of the 1960s, an era which would have come rushing to meet them just as they entered middle age.

The coast path was thick with lush green sea beet and the cement sea-wall was splashed in bright yellow lichen. Feathery sea fennel brushed our legs, and hawthorn banks swelled in full white bloom. We walked the same route from Walton that the Swallows had taken in *Secret Water* on their way back from buying provisions. Walton was, as they had also discovered, further than it looked. Skipper's Island ('Swallow Island'), where the children had pitched camp, was only accessible via the Wade, a causeway submerged at high tide. The Swallows stopped for a nap on their trek back from Walton, reaching the Wade later than planned, and became stranded halfway across by the incoming tide, requiring a last-minute rescue from the Amazons.

The main challenges of camping at Hamford Water involved the mud, which got everywhere. The island turned out to be neither land nor sea, but something in between. J.A. Baker also described his experiences of battling the mud that was to be found coating every part of the tidal Essex below the waterline: 'Mud was deep in the lanes and along the sea-wall; thick ochre mudlike paint; oozing, glutinous mud that seemed to sprout on the marsh, like fungus; octopus mud that clutched and clung and squelched and sucked; slippery mud, smooth and treacherous as oil; mud stagnant; mud evil; mud in the clothes, in the hair, in the eyes; mud to the bone. On the east coast in winter, above or

below the tideline, man walks in water or in mud; there is no dry land. Mud is another element.'

When we reached the Wade, it was entirely submerged. There was no sign of a causeway, and a journey to the island on foot seemed inconceivable. These days Skipper's Island was off-limits in any case, the nature reserve home to a caterpillar that becomes the pretty, brown Fisher's Estuarine Moth. Here it can find its particular diet of rare sea hog fennel. The moth was discovered in 1968 by J.B. Fisher, who lived nearby, and was

found nowhere else in Britain. Visitors are kept out by a warden and the sea by a sea-wall, said to have been built by prisoners during the Napoleonic Wars.

The Backwaters were deserted and beautiful in the raking afternoon sun. At Kirby a miniature quay was overlooked by an ancient black, weather-boarded house, labelled 'The Witch's Quay' by the children in *Secret Water*. A kestrel floated above the path in our eye line, always keeping a hundred yards ahead of us. A scrubbed white little egret swooped over the channel, and we could hear skylarks somewhere up in the banking grey cloud. The top of a red sail slid silently along the creek above the sea-wall. To the left, away over ploughed fields, lay Landermere Hall, and on the estuary another secret quay, Landermere Wharf, where corn, coal and wood from Scandinavia had once been off-loaded.

Eduardo Paolozzi, Nigel Henderson and their respective families moved into adjacent cottages at Landermere Wharf in 1954. Paolozzi was a sculptor from Leith in Edinburgh, his family Italian immigrants, many of whom died when the Arandora Star, a liner carrying Germans and Italians from Britain to Canada, was sunk by a U-boat. He had established his reputation in the avant-garde bastions of Paris and Chelsea, and became one of the principal British movers behind Pop Art. Henderson was best known for his photographs of the East End of London, including Grove Road in Bethnal Green where, 40 years later, Rachel Whiteread cast a life-sized simulacrum of the interior of her demolished terraced house.

The two artists met at the Slade in 1945 and began to design wallpapers and textiles together. When Henderson's wife, Judith, inherited a 16th-century pub, the King's Arms, on the estuary near Thorpe-le-Soken, the friends relocated. In deliberate exile from London, they established the Hammer Prints Ltd workshop, a home-made design operation. However, their designs were the opposite of a cottage industry. They launched a deliberate 'attack on the craft field', embracing mechanical reproduction through screen-printing and photo collage. Their graphics were for use in the home, and drew on eclectic source material, from a 17th-century woodcut pattern they named *Cowcumber* to the everyday objects found in books of early American advertising. In 1956 they created an installation with Brutalist architects Alison and Peter Smithson at *This Is Tomorrow*, the Whitechapel Gallery's definitive 1956 pop art show.

Paolozzi's public mosaics and sculptures defined 1970s London, and his studio is preserved in all its chaotic glory at the Scottish Gallery of Modern Art in Edinburgh. We own a small plaster hand sold cheaply from his studio after his death, the forefinger missing. His work at Hammer Prints tied it all together. The designs he and Henderson produced combined the beginnings of Pop Art with 'art brut', the uninhibited style championed by Jean Dubuffet and characterised by graffiti, children's drawings and mescaline art. Their range, which sold in Liberty's of London, was surreal, unsettling and the exact opposite of the standard 1950s pastel front room. A range of sea-inspired patterns – Barnacle-scape, Crab and Razorshell, Scallop, Sea Urchin – featured in designs that drew on everything that came their way, including the materials surrounding their Essex

workshop. Their work was brewed in splendid isolation in the Backwaters, but was a part of a coming cultural revolution. The combination of the culture of mass production and reproduction with the specificity of this peculiar corner of Essex was unlikely and fascinating. The workshop had closed in the early 1960s as Paolozzi's international commitments took him away more and more, and Hammer Prints ceased production in 1975.

Essex has a history of attracting artists and writers who want to set themselves apart, living close to one another in the

countryside, and sharing ideas and influence. Several 20th-century artists were associated with Great Bardfield and the villages of the Blackwater Valley, inland from Colchester. After artists and their families had first come to live in the area during the 1930s, the Great Bardfield Group was formed, the most famous of whom were the painters and illustrators Edward Bawden and Eric Ravilious. While Ravilious died before his time during the Second World War, the group and its wide range of members continued until the 1960s and included the political cartoonist David Low, costume and set designer Audrey Cruddas, painter John Aldridge and textile and industrial designer Marianne Straub. Later, Grayson Perry spent a traumatic part of his childhood in the village, living in a caravan with his mother and the milkman, with whom she was having an affair.

Landermere Quay, as it is now known, is a short, pretty street featuring a pink, two-storey cottage. It looked to me like the main street of a small but established village, but there was no village. In fact, there was nothing else around at all, apart from ploughed fields with furrows so regular they seemed to shimmer and dissolve into distant, wobbly optical effects. The buildings were ageless, built in a style that seemed to belong to that particular place rather than to any era. The wharf remained, an enclosure of wooden posts and planks around a firmer patch of pebbles than the adjoining beach. We were the only people around, and we felt that we had stepped slightly off the path and away from reality into a floating world.

Unlike the estuaries we had become used to crossing, Landermere Creek came to a sudden stop at Beaumont Quay, turning into a small stream. We reluctantly left the dream-like creek and headed inland to the station at Thorpe-le-Soken. Outside the Thorpe Social Club, a group of men waited on the pavement with a stack of crates containing live pigeons, their business unclear. A silver car honked at us as we walked along the pavement leading to the station – in mockery, suggestion, warning or all three. The village seemed uneasy and we struggled to reconnect from our coastal reveries. The station was dominated by a vast, ruined building, the former Thorpe Maltings. Along with the station hotel it had been fenced off and left to collapse, and it was doing so in spectacular fashion. Such ostentatious neglect seemed menacing. Nevertheless, we booked a date to return, to walk north to Harwich. The end of our expedition was in sight.

X

THE SOKENS

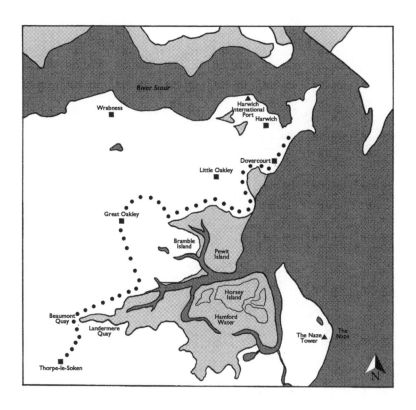

IN THE THREE WEEKS since we had lasted visited Essex, an election had been called, acknowledging the doubt and unease hanging in the air since the previous summer's EU referendum. A pre-planned sequence of events appeared to have been triggered when Clacton's MP, Douglas Carswell, stepped down, declaring himself "UKIP's first and last member of Parliament". His lopsided smile as he announced his mission complete was strangely reminiscent of the England cricketing legend Geoffrey Boycott, who also shared his politics. Shortly afterwards, local elections saw UKIP's support vanish beneath the waves, like the lost church at Walton-on-the-Naze. The political tide that had flooded out of Essex seemed to be ebbing, but it had left the landscape fundamentally altered.

Around the same time, I read about the death of self-declared Glaswegian prophet and painter Benjamin Creme, which had occurred some months before. Known for his regular small ads announcing that the arrival of 'Maitreya, the World Teacher' had already taken place in Kenya in the late 1980s, he lectured for decades on his personal version of the Second Coming. He was an esoteric institution, answering questions about the state of the world in his online magazine, *Share International*, with the help of telepathic messages from the Maitreya. Shortly before his death a letter had been published from Hullbridge, on the Crouch Estuary in Essex, reporting a 'ball of light' of 'a beautiful cherry red colour' in the night sky. Creme had replied to the letter, confirming that this had in fact been a spacecraft from Mars.

The people of eastern Essex have historically been known for their particular approach to religion. Margery Allingham described Essex as 'the puritanical east county, the home of Spurgeon, the nursery of non-conformity.' Charles Spurgeon was a teenaged sensation as a Baptist preacher in the 1850s. He was born in Kelvedon and preached in Colchester before being called, aged 19, to London where he regularly drew crowds 10,000 strong. Essex had its own dissenting church, the Peculiar People, located almost exclusively in south-east Essex. Founded in 1838 by James Banyard, a Rochford farm worker converted from his drunken ways by a Wesleyan service. Their name came from the Bible: 'But ye are a chosen generation, a royal priesthood, an holy nation, a peculiar people.' The Peculiar People were Methodists with some distinctive views of their own, including a preference for prayer over medicine. This led to some of their number being imprisoned after refusing treatment for their children during a diphtheria outbreak in 1910. They have since updated their thinking and image, and are known as the Union of Evangelical Churches. Their chapels still function, not only in Essex towns such as Chelmsford, Southend and Witham, but also in small, obscure villages including Cressing, Daws Heath, Eastwood,

Great Wakering and Little Totham.

Back in Thorpe-le-Soken, we were staying above the Bell Inn, with an excellent view of the adjacent graveyard, where Queen Victoria's physician, Sir William Gull, is buried. Thorpe consists of a single main street with a heavy medieval presence. The 16th-century pub had once been, amongst other things, a guildhall. Thorpe is one of The Sokens, a group of villages that also includes nearby Kirby-le-Soken and Walton-on-the-Naze. They had all formed part of a Saxon peculiar, a group of villages that came under the direct jurisdiction of the King, rather than that of the local diocese. The Sokens had their own ecclesiastical court, which met at Thorpe church until 1861. The Sokens were, I was coming to realise, part of a recurring pattern of enclaves we had encountered along the Essex coast, from semi-detached islands and experimental communities to the social ghettos of Jaywick or Frinton.

Planning our route, we had picked out Thorpe Hall on the map, at the edge of the village. We discovered that it had been the home of Field Marshal Lord Byng, the moustachioed First World War commander, Governor General of Canada and Commissioner of the Metropolitan Police. During the War, plans were drawn up to evacuate Essex in case of invasion. The 1.4 million residents of the county would have been removed to

Oxfordshire, taking only valuables and food. Essex would then have been made inhospitable to the German army, with crops and livestock, food, alcohol, petrol and vehicles destroyed. The plans were never put into operation, but evacuation routes were mapped and an arrow can still be seen on a wall at the inland village of Ugley, designed to direct non-combatants to routes away from main roads.

The village was now hard to fathom. The place had moved on and the hall had been demolished in 2010, replaced by a spa complex called The Lifehouse. We had breakfast in a café housed in an ancient building to a soundtrack of disconcerting, high-energy Europop. Silver four-by-fours jostled for parking bays and a feeling of Sunday morning affluence filled the air.

Behind the high street, the unadopted back lanes carried an air of illicit plotlands development, which reminded me of the collapsing structures of Jaywick. We struck out to the north, heading for Harwich via Beaumont Quay, at the head of Hamford Water. The quay was visited by the children in Ransome's *Secret Water* in their dinghy and is served by a short canal called the Beaumont Cut. We could see the silvery channel it still sliced between the low, grass banks, but the canal had lain disused since before the Second World War. It once connected the Essex farmlands to the sea, via two Thames barges, the Beaumont Belle and the Gleaner, which would leave loaded with hay and return carrying manure. The skeleton of a lighter lay on the opposite side of the creek, decaying among the reeds. The trade, which peaked in the 19th century, involved transporting the manure gathered from the streets of London to Beaumont Quay and other wharves along the Blackwater, for spreading on the fields. The hay grown on these fields was then taken back to London by barge for sale, and converted eventually into manure again. Rev Baring-Gould recorded how 'London muck, that is to say, the sweepings of the London streets, was largely used as manure for the fields, and then the stench was horrible.'

We walked down to the water, where the creek trailed suddenly away and disappeared among a confusion of channels and tiny islands. We scouted the shoreline, but were unable to locate the quay itself. It is reported to have been built with stones recycled from the version of London Bridge demolished in 1831. When the old bridge came down, the Governors of Guy's Hospital had received a share of the materials, some of which were used on their Essex estates. The inscription recording this also seemed to have disappeared, but the connection to Beaumont Quay was via one William Gull, who had been brought up in Thorpe and was a lecturer at Guy's. Gull was the son of a wharfinger and was born on a barge moored at St Osyth. He became the pre-eminent doctor of his age, famous for saving the Prince of Wales during a near-fatal attack of typhoid. The nation hung for weeks on the bulletins posted at local police stations with the latest updates on the prince's condition and, when he recovered, Gull was knighted in thanks. However, he had acquired a more dubious afterlife through his supposed role in the Jack the Ripper saga, cast as a predator who descended on the East End in a blacked-out coach. He was a central figure in the conspiracy theory created by Joseph

Gorman, a fantasist who claimed to be Walter Sickert's illegitimate son, which also involved Freemasons, the Royal Family and a secret Catholic heir to the throne. He first told his story in the early 1970s, resulting in a BBC mini-series, although he later retracted it as a hoax.

The shore beyond Beaumont Quay was inaccessible, occupied by something marked on the map, with calculated vagueness, as 'Works'. So, instead, we climbed inland above Hamford Water, where cement roads led us across fields. We

were unable to identify the elegant black sea birds, with white underbellies, banking over the water. A low mist lay over the tidal flats. The Naze Tower stood both tall and tiny against the horizon. The ground was baked hard as cement.

At Great Oakley Church we stumbled across a memorial to the six children and their teacher who were killed in a bus accident in the Essex countryside in 1978. A cottage on the main street featured a full-sized concrete pill box, incongruously occupying its front garden along with an apple tree. It was as though the village was waiting to star in *It Happened Here*, the 1964 film that imagined life in Britain under the Nazis. If the German army had slipped along Hamford Water under cover of darkness, Great Oakley would have been the first occupied village in England. The day was becoming hotter, and the mist thinning down to a persistent haze. At the Little Oakley pub where we stopped for lunch, the landlady and her mother told us about the various ghosts inhabiting the bar, which was otherwise occupied by pensioners. Their accounts were matter of fact, as though describing an entirely material phenomenon. They even claimed to have brought one ghost with them when they moved from the pub at Great Oakley.

Rev Sabine Baring-Gould left among his papers a short, unpublished manuscript in which he recorded his personal experience of 'the occult'. He writes of a night in his Mersea house, sitting by an open fire with 'a friend, now dead, a solicitor of Colchester'. The solicitor had leapt to his feet, alarmed by 'a sound as of someone walking from behind the settle, the length of the hall, drawing a stiff satin dress along the oak-polished floor.' On another evening, alone at home past midnight, with the moon shining through the window, Baring-Gould was 'startled by a harsh burst of laughter, close in my ear' in an otherwise empty house.

The landlady and her mother also shed some light on the 'Works', a complex of factories marked in particularly vague way on all available maps. We were unsure what it could be, but locally there was no secret. The site was a long-standing explosives factory and testing site that occupied the entirety of the tidal Bramble Island. Securely fenced from the public it was owned by a company called Exchem. Its website carried an advert for the forthcoming Security and Counter-Terror Expo at Excel, in London. We regained the sea-wall alongside barbed wire and signs warning of prosecutions under the Explosives Acts of 1875 and 1923.

Bramble Island was flooded on Black Monday, 1897, the sea-wall breached and its sheep drowned. Shortly after this, it was bought by the High Explosives Company as a suitably remote location for manufacturing. Explosives were produced there throughout the 20th century, despite several fatal explosions and further disastrous flooding. The 1928 flood, which had swept down the Thames and swamped Westminster, damaged the factory and led to the permanent abandonment of Garnham Island to the south, now framed by trace remnants of sea-walls. In 1950, three workers died in an explosion. Then, during the Great Flood of 1953, floodwater washed through the factory, drowning the night watchman. His body was recovered, days later, 10 miles

up the coast. The flood washed away 40 wooden buildings and 150 tons of explosive, some of which later came in on the tide in Margate. The incredibly dangerous clean-up operation involved collecting the lost explosives on a barge and dumping them out at sea near the Cork Light Vessel, where they are still, even today, marked by a warning buoy.

The tide was out, far out, leaving a temporary mosaic of dark brown and acid green. The saltings concealed Pewit Island, on the far reaches of Hamford Water, marked on the Swallows'

map as 'Pewitland'. Since their maps, it has merged almost completely with the sea, with no defences to keep the water out, and is submerged at every tide. It too was irretrievably flooded in the Black Monday flood of 1897, which split the island in two and turned the southern half into New Island.

We approached Harwich through a waist-high tunnel of rank-smelling weeds. The sea defences hardened and the shore became an unforgiving concrete promenade. The leading lights at Dovercourt appeared beside the long beach, a pair of cast iron Victorian lighthouses which once marked the entrance to the navigable shipping channel leading to ports on the Stour and Orwell estuaries. Beyond, the breakwater overlooked by the Beacon Hill Battery, topped with a disused Second World War radar tower. Further away still, the gantry cranes of the Port of Felixstowe loomed close, just a mile across the estuary by ferry, but many miles by land, and in Suffolk. The Stour is also a cultural boundary, and has a different accent and a different name on each bank. The river is pronounced "Stower" in Essex, but less than a mile on the Suffolk shore the same water is the "Stoor".

We detoured between post-war semis looking for the Harwich Redoubt, a fort built to guard against Napoleon which is shaped like a partially buried doughnut. It was tucked behind gardens full of residents enjoying the hot afternoon listening to a compilation of Andrew Lloyd Webber's greatest hits, or so it seemed to me. From the fort we could see out across the Medusa Channel, named after Nelson's frigate.

We climbed inland towards our end point, the station at Harwich Town, and entered Dovercourt, on the southern outskirts of the port. In his novel *The Prime Minister*, Anthony Trollope described Dovercourt as 'a not sufficiently well-known marine paradise,' a retreat for Ferdinand Lopez, a financial adventurer doomed to ruin. The town park, raised above the promenade beach huts, is the site of Cliff House, built by East India Company merchant John Bagshawe, who had overstretched himself attempting to develop Dovercourt as a spa town. His bankruptcy led to the demolition of his mansion; and the library, conservatory, grottos and gardens of the spa were long-vanished, leaving the town with a frayed edge.

Harwich is pressed onto a narrow peninsula. We found it almost deserted. When we encountered a fellow visitor she, like us, was confused at the lack of the facilities usually associated with a town. Together, we located the only cashpoint, hidden in a shop that appeared at first glance to be boarded up. The centre of Harwich felt ancient and was indeed based on a medieval layout, with many of its original houses intact. It seemed to have been in a long, slow decline for the previous century and more. Writing in

1931, Clifford Bax quoted a local, unnamed guidebook which he claimed described the town as 'a pitiful example of a decayed port ... a half-ruined town of narrow, dismal streets, honeycombed with squalid alleys.' The downfall of the town was blamed on the relocation of the ferry port to Parkeston, some distance from the town to the west, where it was still to be found. Harwich peaked as a port in the pre-industrial era. It was the probable departure point for The Mayflower, which left for the New World in 1620. George III's queen-to-be, Charlotte of Mecklenburg, arrived at

Harwich from Germany in 1761, after a voyage lasting more than two weeks, on a journey to her wedding in London. Her body returned from Harwich by boat, 57 years later, for burial in her home country. The Royal Naval Dockyard was downgraded in 1713, and the Navy left in 1823, returning temporarily during the Napoleonic War and the two World Wars, times of threat along the entire Essex coast. In November 1918, the German U-boat fleet surrendered to the British navy at Harwich following the Armistice. At least 120 U-boats arrived at the port, where they

were boarded by the Navy and their crews taken off, before being tied up in a line in the Stour two miles long.

In the centre of Harwich, the first election posters we had seen for Labour in Essex appeared in windows. The seat had a Labour MP at the height of the New Labour surge, but redrawn boundaries had merged the town with the surrounding north Essex countryside. It was now part of a constituency represented for a generation by Bernard Jenkin, a Conservative MP who had spent his political career opposing EU membership. We planned to return to Harwich soon, before the General Election, to complete our journey. Only one day's walk remained before we would reach the county boundary at Manningtree, and the end of the Essex coast path.

XI

STOUR

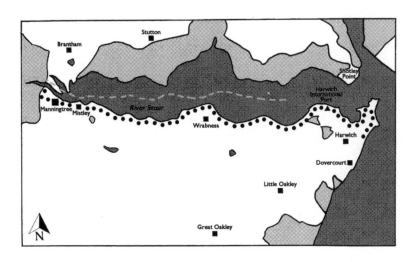

THE WEEKEND BEFORE THE ELECTION there was increased tension in the air. The polls showed the gap between the Conservatives and Labour closing. The Prime Minister seemed ill at ease and her party tactically inept. Voters were taking notice, but change was not in the air. There was little expectation of anything other than a large Conservative majority. We decided to return to Essex for the final leg of our walk, following the Stour Estuary back inland all the way from Harwich to the county boundary at Manningtree.

The journey east was slow and halting, the weather unpredictable. A flash flood on the edges of London stopped every train and a restless crowd filled Liverpool Street Station. Departure boards in meltdown, we wrestled with travel permutations. Essex suddenly appeared much further away from London than usual. The rail app on my phone informed me, 'You cannot plan a journey in the past.' Eventually we reached Manningtree, but missed the hourly connection on the branch line to Harwich. A group of stranded passengers grumbled and looked on as the sky darkened and a storm of epic proportions inched towards us. The station bar was closed but three locals had set up an impromptu lock-in. They gestured apologetically to us through the window from behind their pints, doors firmly closed.

Three and a half hours later we reached Dovercourt at the edge of Harwich. We stayed in a friendly B&B above the Dovercourt Job Centre. The next morning, the storm had passed. In 1954, Nikolas Pevsner wrote, 'Although present-day Harwich might well be called the poor relation of Dovercourt, it is pleasant to look at and wander in whereas Dovercourt is not.' His observation was caustic, but accurate. The Dovercourt we encountered was down-at-heel with neglected terraces, collapsing buildings and large houses chopped into tiny flats. A towering pile of bin bags swarmed with sparrows. A car lay half buried in a driveway filled with drifts of poppies.

We circled the deserted streets of Harwich, where Tudor sea captains might just have stepped out of sight, around the corner. The prospect across Harwich Harbour revealed the Shotley peninsular and the container cranes at Felixstowe, apparently within touching distance across the narrow strait that channelled the Stour into the North Sea. The previous week a 40-foot minke whale had washed up dead on Felixstowe beach. This episode echoed the strange happenings of Sarah Perry's novel *The Essex Serpent*, a book which was everywhere that spring. Its story of palaeontology, Victorian women and illicit passion stirring under clerical surplices was set in a remote village on the Blackwater. A dead man found by the estuary reawakens the dormant folk tale of a winged serpent which emerges from the sea. The book had unexpectedly brought the Essex marshes into the zeitgeist, or the other way around. It seemed to fulfil a desire for visions of the present reflected, reassuringly, in an equally disquieting past. Monsters lurking off the coast had manifested for centuries in a cycle of retreat and return, and would melt away as suddenly as they had appeared.

The sea monster had a real-life counterpoint. Jules Pretty reported that in the autumn of 1954, and again the following summer, bloated corpses had washed up near Dead Man's Bay on Canvey Island, where the sea is said to return those it has swallowed. These bodies were different though: dark brown, equipped with gills and too small to be human. A witness told him they were just angler fish, but the tale soon became something much more in the telling. People on this coast are unsurprised by the appearance of something from the sea that is neither man nor fish, but a bit of both. It mirrors the status of much of coastal Essex as a hinterland, now mud, now water, enabled by a sea-wall that has been in place for centuries, but could only ever be temporary.

Not only was Harwich empty, but it seemed to have no expectation of visitors. The only shop we could find was the one we had visited before, still reluctantly open. It was the final weekend of election campaigning but the town's UKIP office, decked out with Union Jacks and attack posters depicting Theresa May as a 'con artist' in a burglar mask, was closed. A vast Stena

Line ferry, the size of a cruise ship, slid silently behind a 17th-century Harwich street, en route to the Hook of Holland. It passed the Navyard where men-of-war were once built and where Samuel Pepys, as Secretary to the Navy, worried in his diary about Dutch ships harrying the east coast. The Navyard had opened in 1652, at the start of the first Anglo-Dutch War, and was on the frontline of all four wars with the Dutch fought during the 17th and 18th centuries. It was a ship-building yard, and a sign on its perimeter fence recorded the Men of War constructed there, from the ships of the 1660s – the Roebuck, the Rupert, the Swiftsure, the Resolution – to the enormous, 90-gun wooden warships the Albermarle and the Sandwich, and the final two commissions, a pair of gunboats built shortly before the yard closed in 1827.

The Navyard occupied a site of strategic importance for more than a thousand years, commanding the mouth of the Haven, a deep, natural harbour at the confluence of the Rivers Stour and Orwell. The narrow defensible entrance, with little more than a mile separating Harwich from Felixstowe, had made it a natural location for shipping for centuries. In 885AD the River Stour marked the boundary between Wessex, ruled by Alfred the Great, and the Danelaw (the part of England controlled by the Vikings). At the Battle of Stourmouth, a fleet sent up the Essex coast by King Alfred was defeated by 'pirates', as the Anglo-Saxon chronicle described the Danes. Bloody Point, on the Suffolk shore at Shotley, opposite Harwich, perhaps commemorates this battle.

Leaving Harwich behind, we passed the operational headquarters of Trinity House, the charity responsible for lighthouses, pilots and navigational aids in British waters. Its storage yard was filled with rolling hills of shiny, slithering, black chain and stacks of buoys, which looked entirely different out of water. At sea, without no objects to provide scale, they seemed small. On land, they were the same scale as the hulls of the ships they protected – heavy steel balloons, cages taller than a person, painted in bright yellows, greens and reds, some marked with their previous locations: Black Deep, Rye Fairway, Flamborough, London Sand Outer. The Swallows, in Arthur Ransome's other East Anglian book, *We Didn't Mean to Go to Sea*, had a close encounter with one of these. Losing their anchor and drifting from their Harwich mooring in the dark on a borrowed boat, The Goblin, they narrowly escaped being crushed against a square-caged buoy marking shoals, somewhere in the direction of the Cork Light Vessel. The largest structures were blue and yellow wreck marker buoys, extra tall and topped with a yellow crucifix. They looked like Las Vegas wedding chapels. Samuel Pepys had worked here too as Master of Trinity House and his local connections were deepl. He eventually became MP for Harwich, the culmination of his long career in the civil service.

In a 1960s estate on the fringes of Harwich we spotted one lone election canvasser, knocking on doors in Dovercourt in a red tie and getting no replies. He was highly conspicuous, the only man in town wearing a suit, but there was no evidence, beyond the tie, to show which party he belonged to. Beyond the houses, the coast path became a greenway among industry and recent housing, lodged awkwardly between the railway and the Stour. Elderflower was in full bloom, and the Dovercourt sparrows ranged out among the bushes. The village of Parkeston, at the approach to the ferry terminal, was marked by the abandoned church St Paul's, which had the character of a missionary station. A cross of Easter flowers tied to the railings outside had dried almost to dust.

The Harwich ferry terminal is more closely linked to the Netherlands than anywhere else in Britain. Mail boats began a service across the North Sea to Holland in 1661, taking passengers along with the post. The route fell into decline after the captains proved reluctant to switch from sail to steam, and the mail service moved to Dover, taking the shorter route to Calais instead. Later, the port refused to expand to accommodate larger steamers, marking the end of its heyday.

The cliffs over the Stour were eaten back from the river

and obscured by vegetation. They had been dug away for cement stone, exceptionally valuable and sought after in the early 19th century. The invention of Roman cement in the 1790s, using deposits found in the London Clay cliffs either side of the Stour, turned Harwich into the centre of the cement industry. Exceptionally strong, Roman cement was sold across Britain and northern Europe and was used to build Regency London, used for example in the stucco rendering found on John Nash's houses. Five cement works were based around in the town and an estimated one million tons of stone removed from the cliffs. The entire Harwich headland became severely eroded and the practice was banned, after which the stone was dredged at sea instead with a fleet of 300 smacks working offshore by 1850. By the 1870s the rise of Portland cement had ended the Harwich boom.

Beyond the ferries, a fenced path led past a compound occupied by oil storage tanks and a notice warning of explosions. This was the Halterman Carless refinery ('Fuelling the pace of today's world'). The smell of crude oil as we passed through the compound was strong, sweet and heavy. Then the long stretch of industrial coast ended abruptly and we were in the Essex countryside again. A man equipped with a stick and a strong Suffolk accent offered us directions. He pointed us up the hill for the best views of the Stour and what he described as "the Mickey

Mouse House".

We did as he suggested and climbed a ridge to look out over green fields of wheat and a wide sweep of water to a spectacular building on the opposite bank of the Stour, its long wings balanced with a tall, central clock tower. This is the Royal Hospital School which, while still a school, no longer trains boys for the navy. It is, however, home to relics of the HMS Ganges, a training ship which had become a shore-bound naval school based nearby at Shotley. In *Secret Water*, the Swallows' father,

Commander Walker, is summoned to HMS Ganges, leaving them to camp on their own at Hamford Water. Although never explicitly stated, the book was published in 1939 and its events seem to take place in the run up the Second World War, so it was no surprise that Commander Walker would have been in demand. The childhood summers of the Essex coast disguised a world on the brink of disaster. HMS Ganges was decommissioned in 1976, but the outsized, androgynous figure of an Indian boy in white robe, crown and ropes of pearls, carved for its figurehead in the

Bombay Dockyard, was an imposing reminder.

Something even more unlikely was at hand. We passed through Wrabness and along a drive that led to a house that appeared to us like a vision, the most unlikely building in the county. It sat at the end of the main street in at Wrabness, out on its own in a field, looking highly eccentric. It had the gilt roof of a Russian Orthodox Church and the green and white checkerboard tiles of a gingerbread house. Each tile was embossed with strange, naïve symbols and the roof was capped with a huge diamond-patterned urn and the metal figure of a naked, pregnant women with a bob. *A House for Essex* was designed by the artist Grayson Perry and the architect Charles Holland. Completed in 2015, it is a holiday cottage like no other. It is an attempt to create a new Essex vernacular in the form of a shrine to a fictional, pregnant woman called Julie – an architecture designed to elevate the ordinary to the extraordinary. It has attracted comment and visitors from far and wide. Indeed, at the end of our walk we ran into someone we knew at Manningtree Station, with a group of cyclists who had come all the way from London to see it.

Until the 1960s, Wrabness was the location for the Royal Naval Mine Depot, but no trace remains and the site has returned to nature. Wrabness itself has another structure, older but almost as strange: a wooden cage in the churchyard containing a large bell, built after the church tower collapsed in the 17th century. We passed from village to woods, then we were back on an empty shore path, larks climbing, passing the hidden beaches of Jacques Bay. For the first time in many miles there was sand at low tide, and no wall to separate land from sea.

On the other side of the woods, we arrived in Mistley, a village with a prosperous air. It contained, we discovered, a quay and a malt extract works, both of which were, surprisingly, still in operation. The quay, however, was behind temporary fencing, and we had to divert off the river. In a café we read press cuttings about a local conflict with the port owners over access. The owners, a company called Trent Wharfage, had fenced the previously public quay in 2008 and a 'Free the Quay' protest had been held every year since. The campaigners had recently won a court case, but the situation was still unresolved. Despite the disquiet, the river traffic and alluringly green tidal flats of the Stour Estuary provided a fine backdrop, a combination of working and natural landscape that is becoming increasingly rare in Britain.

On the edge of Mistley, two 18th-century baroque towers stood apart in a graveyard, their purpose unclear, but carrying for me the occult atmosphere of a Nicholas Hawksmoor church. The Mistley Towers are the remains of the demolished church of St Mary the Virgin, designed by Robert Adam and commissioned in a failed attempt to reinvent Mistley as a spa town.

The local MP, Richard Ridley, became a rich man when George III appointed him Paymaster General of the Forces in 1768. First, he commissioned new gardens for his house, Mistley Hall, full of Chinese and Gothic follies. Then he brought in Adam to rebuild the church and install a saltwater bath. The latter never happened, and the nave of the new church was pulled down, leaving just the towers. They were, as Pevsner put it, 'far from religious-looking.' Now they haunt the approaches to the village,

presiding over the graveyard where the Witchfinder General, Matthew Hopkins, is buried. Essex had a reputation for witches. Canewdon, a village on the Crouch in the Essex Archipelago has been described, according to folk historian Charlotte Mason, as 'the witch country' because there were always six witches there, 'three in silk, three in cotton.'

The appalling events of the witch hunt originated right here by the Stour. Matthew Hopkins was born in Suffolk and is thought to have inherited a sum which allowed him to buy

the Thorn Inn at Mistley and set up as a gentleman. The two-year crusade, which involved Hopkins and the Suffolk landowner John Stearne, began in Manningtree in March 1644, when Stearne claimed to have overheard a group of women talking about meeting the Devil. Their first accusations resulted in the execution of 19 women at Chelmsford, while a further three died in prison. Hopkins and Stearne extracted confessions using notorious interrogations techniques such as 'pricking' with knives and needles to discover 'invisible marks' and 'swimming', which involved tying a woman to a chair and dropping her in water to see whether she floated, the sign of a witch. Their interrogations were conducted mostly in Mistley and Manningtree, but the pair travelled across East Anglia, accompanied by a team of women who carried out the 'pricking'. By the time their techniques were questioned by local justices, 300 women are believed to have been executed on evidence they provided, a number that accounts for more than half of all known executions for witchcraft in Britain. Despite being most familiar as a grey-bearded Vincent Price in Michael Reeves' 1968 film *Witchfinder General*, Hopkins was no older than 28 when he died in 1647, shortly after retiring from his adopted profession.

We were now within reach of the Essex county boundary at Manningtree. Larger than Mistley, the town seemed equally well-to-do. According to *Highways and Byways in Essex*, in 1931 'the town offered a variety of pleasures – fishing, cricket, bowls, lawn tennis, hunting, and shooting,' but not yachting, as the Stour became difficult to navigate that far upstream. Manningtree was therefore virtually the only Essex coastal town without a culture of yachts and pleasure boats. The Stour Estuary was still broad, however, and its marshy setting made it unmistakably an Essex river.

Passing through the town centre, we encountered the face of Bernard Jenkin the long-serving local MP, on posters in the window of his constituency office. In 1993 he had been one of the group described by Prime Minister John Major as "bastards" in a leaked recording after they had failed to vote with the government to ratify the Maastricht Treaty. In the same conversation, Major had characterised the anti-Maastricht campaigners as "the dispossessed and the never-possessed." The Eurosceptic wing saw itself as a group of outsiders within the Conservative party and was dominated by east of England MPs, with an Essex hardcore of Iain Duncan Smith (Chingford), Nicholas Bonsor (Upminster), Teresa Gorman (Billericay), Teddy Taylor (Southend-on-Sea), John Whittingdale (Colchester South and Maldon) and Jenkin himself. Nearly a generation has passed since their moment of fame and they have become largely forgotten, superseded by a new generation of UKIP-aligned right-wingers who have gone further than their predecessors had dared in their attacks on immigration. However, the process they started had lasted beyond their time, and had led directly to the Brexit vote. Their successors are Cabinet ministers and media personalities, rather than fringe malcontents.

We walked along the industrial fringe of Manningtree, hugging the river. The county boundary was marked on a road bridge halfway across the Stour. Suffolk is the most easterly English

county and its coat of arms shows a sun rising over water. The last in a line of pill boxes marking out the full 350 miles of Essex coastline was strategically positioned where the county came to an end. Beyond, the bridge sheds and backyards came to an abrupt stop and Dedham Vale lay beyond, a carefully preserved pastoral setting that was insistently described in tourist marketing material as 'Constable Country'.

In the weeks that followed, a quick succession of era-defining

events occurred. A bomb in Manchester brought grim scenes of terror that have long been feared in Britain. The sense of instability was confirmed shortly afterwards when news footage showed two men, faces covered, strolling through Borough Market on the south bank of the Thames in London, casually and randomly stabbing strangers.

Shortly afterwards, the General Election brought a result no one had predicted. The Brexit mandate sought by the Prime Minister failed to materialise and, instead, a version of the future began to unfurl that had seemed impossible days earlier. UKIP vanished from the map like the Essex mudflats under a flood tide, its policies seamlessly subsumed by the Conservative party. Labour outsider Jeremy Corbyn came to the threshold of government, kept out only by the widely resented support of the Democratic Unionist Party of Northern Ireland, the only group of politicians in Britain that almost everyone else agreed were crazy. The government which, a few months ago, was settling in for a full five-year term, had bypassed its own legislation on fixed term parliaments to, as it turned out, obliterate its own majority. It seemed impossible that the Prime Minister could last for more than a few weeks, or that the government would survive the gruelling Brexit negotiations to come. David Cameron had blithely imagined that a vote would settle disagreements once and for all, but it had simply solidified differences and made it impossible to resolve. The Conservative party's own MPs, deeply divided, would never agree on what the vote actually means.

The party of order, continuity, economic responsibility and the establishment, had been caught up in its own myths. The story of political isolation, a nation strongest when battling alone, had taken hold and was now read as literal truth. Now characters emerged into mainstream politics who seemed to be parodies from a fictionalised past: the chump, Boris Johnson; the toff, Jacob Rees-Mogg; the cad, Nigel Farage.

Finally, a week later and worst of all, a tower block fire in Latimer Grove became a catastrophe of a kind not seen for years. The horrifying number of victims stripped the civilised facade from systems of regulation and government. The fire joined a succession of modern disasters so beyond the ordinary that they were known by a single place-name: Aberfan, Hillsborough, Lockerbie and now Grenfell. The blackened ruin scarring the London skyline was impossible to ignore, ever-present in the background of what had once been ordinary views.

XII

ARCHIPELAGO

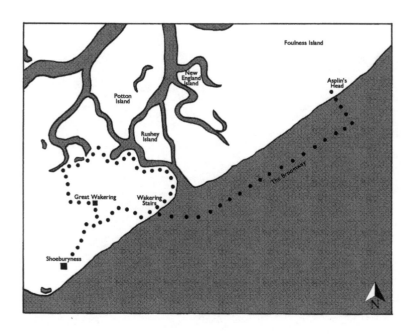

ALTHOUGH WE HAD REACHED the county boundary at Manningtree, we were not finished with Essex. There was a gap in our journey. The Foulness Ranges, closed for military exercises after the summer attacks in Manchester and London, occupied seven miles of the Essex coast. The island of Foulness, farmland among low-lying salt marsh, was firmly off-limits and there was no possibility of walking the Broomway tidal path. The landscape has been military land for generations, and on Foulness ordinary life was beyond living memory. It is, like large areas of Britain, frozen in the first half of the 20th century, access controlled by military security. These zones are noticed by few, a shadow Britain.

As 2017 came to an end, I concentrated on finishing my account of our walk. Essex County Cricket Club won the County Championship for the first time since the 1980s. But nothing else had been resolved; uncertainty had become a default state of existence. Two years of national turmoil were proving to be just the beginning, and with no end in sight.

Then, in June 2018, an email arrived from Brian and Toni Groom, the couple who led occasional walks along The Broomway. They had intended to retire in 2017, but were organising one last trip for the people who had missed out the year before. The timing was perfect. Jo and I cancelled our plans and arrived at the foot of The Broomway one Saturday lunchtime, Wellington boots in our rucksacks, to complete the final, missing piece of the puzzle.

The Essex archipelago was a mysterious place long before the Ministry of Defence took possession of Foulness and the surrounding islands in 1915. The year before, Arnold Bennett had described it as though it was, in fact, the heart of darkness imagined from Conrad's Thames Estuary: 'At low water the entire Christian era is reduced to nothing, in many a creek of the Colne, the Blackwater, and the Stour; England is not inhabited; naught has been done; the pristine reigns as perfectly as in the African jungle.' The Archipelago consists of six islands south of the River Crouch, a slab of land split into marshy fragments by its tributary, the River Roach. In 1889, *The Spectator* described the islands as 'rich deep-clodded lands.' Of the islands – Wallasea, Potton, Rushley, New England, Havengore, and Foulness – the latter is by far the largest. Only Rushley and Wallasea, site of the RSPB's saltmarsh remodelling, are not in the possession of the Ministry of Defence. Rushley is privately owned and can be reached only by boat or via a low tide ford, reported to be very muddy. New England Island seemed to have been lost to the sea after the 'Black Monday' floods of 1897, but was repaired by the War Department in 1915 to provide a stable route to Foulness.

The *Spectator* article reads like a report from an expedition to chart a foreign land: 'The islands differ in size and cultivation of land. Potton is quite inland, and does not touch the sea. Wallasea, between the Crouch and the Roach, is now connected with the main-land by a causeway. The smallest is Rushley; it and New England and Havengore are mere single farms, mainly pasturage, the latter owned and occupied by a local squire.'

The landscape of the Archipelago provided the setting for Sylvia Townsend Warner's novel *The True Heart*, published in 1927. It is a story of the marshes and the orphaned Sukey, packed off to a position as a servant girl in a remote farm on an island. Her benefactor and then enemy, Mrs Seaborn, has a name that suggests the confusion between physical states – solid and liquid – inherent in the marsh landscape. Where the landscape becomes uncertain, so do the boundaries between the real and the imagined, and between interpretations of right and wrong. The farm at Derryman's Island, like the underworld, could only be reached by ferry. In the book, the saltings are being claimed back from the sea and 'put under the plough', but when the sea fog rolls in, 'flowing over it, billowing in like the sea's ghost come back to claim its own ... Small wonder that she felt astray from her proper self.'

Warner had visited the Archipelago on impulse. Like Jack London, who had begun his 'expedition' into the uncharted East

End 'abyss' in Stanford's Covent Garden bookshop, Warner found her connection to Essex in a map department. She ventured east in July 1922, drawn towards the strange coastline she saw on a map in the stationery department at Whiteleys, Bayswater: 'The green marsh on the map pleased me, and the blue creeks and the marsh names.' Disembarking from the train at Shoeburyness, the end of the line, she took a bus to Great Wakering and then walked out onto the marshes until she ran out of land somewhere among the maze of tidal creeks separating Foulness from the mainland. She was forced to seek shelter from the rain in a farmhouse. We took the same route, taking a bus to Landwick, a set of cottages at the edge of the military land managed by QinetiQ.

The bus took us through the spread of houses that had grown from Southend out east during the second half of the 20th century. At Thorpe Bay, even two-storey houses were disguised as bungalows, to fit the retirement atmosphere. North Shoebury was a baffling tangle of 2000s cul-de-sacs, as detached from their surroundings as the firing range. The accelerated development of south-east Essex has been a source of contention for years. At Barling, the last village before the Archipelago, a newly built house was set on fire in 1988. 'Was it a last, despairing protest at the blatant, brash invasion of this peaceful place?' asked Essex author Stan Jarvis at the time, lamenting the change brought to

Barling by 'the age of the car'.

The transition from high density Southend to the remote coast was physically short, but psychically demanding. The driver of the bus ahead had abandoned the journey and pulled over, suffering from a panic attack. At the QinetiQ guardhouse, we slipped past a barrier onto a road through fields of soft, green wheat.

In 1894, *The Spectator* recorded that '[a]ll the draught of the country-side goes by "The Brooms." A singular highway this, repaired by no Board, and minded by no waywarden, stretching for seven miles to Fishermen's Head, near the point of Foulness, along the level sands half a, mile out at sea, marked every twenty yards by bundles of Brooms fixed firmly in the sand and rising a foot above.' The Broomway can only have been inconsistently marked, as it took 400 brooms to cover the entire route and, although locals were paid to replace them, they were washed away by the tide.

The route, sometimes known as 'The Doomway', is notoriously dangerous in the wrong conditions. The path is the only firm route across the sands, but is unmarked. The tide comes in at different rates depending on the time of year. In clear visibility it is beautiful, but the weather can change very fast, leaving a walker with no clue to their direction. The church at Churchend, on Foulness, records the deaths of 66 people drowned on the Broomway, including local residents who regularly walked the path, but were caught out nonetheless.

We met Brian and Toni at Wakering Stairs, a notch in the sea-wall overlooked by an MoD watchtower. After we had all slid into our boots, they led us, a disparate group of 10, straight out to sea, in the direction signalled by a red footpath arrow. The causeway at Wakering Stairs was just a strip of rock that trailed out into the

sands. Alongside the rocks the remains of wattles could be seen, laid to form a solid surface, some carbon-dated to the early 17th century. The tide was at its lowest point, and the sands stretched out further than we could see. Far away, a woman walked her dogs close to the wreck of the Pisces, a fishing protection boat that had run aground in the 1970s. We walked along a path that was no longer apparent in any way. There was only firm sand covered in a thin layer of sea water, splashing our boots. The only landmark was a patch of cordgrass, a small, lush lawn surrounded by acres of

mud, where we turned north-east to walk parallel with the coast. The Broomway had shifted, and the route we now walked was further from Foulness than it had been a few years earlier. Brian explained that he and Toni had once tried cutting off the corner, and found themselves floundering across a mile of soft sand that pulled at their boots.

Maplin Sands covered an area twice as large as Foulness, land continually in transition to sea, sea in transition to land. The edge wobbled in the far distance, impossible for us make

out. A mirage occluded the horizon line, doubling the container ships anchored in the Thames Estuary and the gas storage tanks on the Isle of Grain in Kent. Also mirrored on the horizon was a dark line which, Brian told us, was an artificial island. It had been constructed in the early 1970s as an experiment to test whether permanent structures could survive on the sands. It was now in a state of slow collapse. This was the first of several, failed attempts to build a new London airport in the Thames Estuary, following the Roskill Commission of 1971.

Foulness kept a low profile on our western side, but strange objects protruded above its skyline. Brian told us that the mast we could see, tilted at 45 degrees, was used to test airplane ejector seats. Two taller masts, which guarded the northern tip of the island, carried sensors. Projectiles were fired between them onto the sands to collect data on their performance. These twin masts were the tallest structures on the island, and the largest in sight since the demolition of the chimney at the Isle of Grain power station, once a useful landmark for those on The Broomway.

According to Jules Pretty, Foulness is still used for 'all kinds of secret stuff: weapons development and testing, the destruction of ammunition, more atomic testing.' The Atomic Weapons Establishment had a branch on Foulness, although its staff had moved out when QinetiQ arrived in 1997. It is the perfect site for testing bombs and missiles, which can be fired into the sea and their remains retrieved from the sands when the tide is out. Test firing takes place from the north-eastern tip of the island onto the long nose of Maplin Sands, but is only possible during clear weather conditions, not least because cloud cover amplifies explosions, which can be heard across much of south-east Essex. During firing, low frequency booms cross the islands, with a sound described by Jules Pretty as 'eyeball wobbling'. Brian explained that the island had been used for high-level security projects including a full-scale reconstruction of a fully loaded 747 following the Lockerbie air crash, to test the impact of a bomb in the hold. The armoured front door and windows of 10 Downing Street have also been tested for bomb resistance on Foulness.

Foulness is a truly remote place. Ken Worpole reported that the women of Foulness wore Dutch costume until the First World War, with stronger connections to their sister landscape in the Netherlands than to mainland Britain. Margery Allingham's sister, Emily, described Foulness as '1837 not 1937 ... We have oil lamps and the roads except for the one cement road through the place are deep ruts ... like Mersea used to be before the war.' By 1949, however, S. L. Bensusan claimed that all traces of the marsh dialect that was the basis of his popular stories had gone – 'Today you will listen in vain for any prolonged echo from the past' – along with the culture of the island people.

Foulness remains separate, nevertheless. I had first heard of it while watching Simon Stephens's 2006 play *Motortown* at the Royal Court Theatre in London, where the island symbolises the mental disconnection imposed by war. The play is about the gulf between London, where well-to-do Hampstead couples look for sexual kicks with angry young men, and Essex, well-stocked with the latter. Danny, a squaddie, brings the horrors of Iraq back with him from his tour of duty. His mates hope he can get them onto

Foulness, 'The Island', but once you cross the creek, you are not coming back.

We were now aiming for a marker post, the closest to the shore, one of three along Havengore Creek. At low tide there was no creek to speak of, just a tall wooden pole with crossbeams, hung with reflectors, like a sunken mast from the SS Richard Montgomerie. On the featureless sands it appeared grotesquely oversized. We moved on, entering a Broomway trance, through a place that was more and more enticing. The sun was high, but

a light coastal breeze cooled us. The sky swept from horizon to horizon, and the light reflected off the watery surface under our feet. Robert Macfarlane described the Broomway as 'certainly the unearthliest path I have ever walked.' We were truly in a provisional land, a place that would be gone in three hours. Nothing could be simpler, or deadlier, than to walk east, straight out towards the North Sea across the endless surface. When the tide turned it would cover the flat sands faster than running pace.

We reached Asplins Head, the furthest point of our

walk. A watchtower overlooked the jetty, which had a semi-circular concrete wall around its north side. This, we learnt, was the remnants of an experimental structure used by the MoD to contain experiments that involved setting fire to liquified gas. The site had a ritual appearance, a blazing circle drawn on the sands. The ground was not as firm as it appeared. A tank had once driven confidently out onto the beach at Asplins Head and sunk to the chassis. Hundreds of lugworms curled over the smooth, runnelled mud, indistinguishable from their casts. Pools of water contained tiny crabs, which scuttled off sideways and burrowed out of sight at our approach.

We turned to retrace our route back to Wakering Stairs, walking into the sun. The light made the sands shine, and their bright reflective surface was liquid and pin sharp. The full sky dome around and over us was flecked with wispy, white cloud. As I walked, peering at the mud under my feet, my focus jumped and the solid surface melted away to be replaced by the sky. It no longer stopped at the horizon, but rolled both over my head and all the way beneath my feet. The ground dissolved and I walked across the surface of a mirror, where there was no surface at all. The Broomway crossed neither land nor sea, but formed a bridge between both. The doubled horizon marked a vanishing point where reflection met object, and it no longer mattered which was which.

The morning after we returned from the Broomway I woke, for the first time in my life, with the unmistakable symptoms of hay fever. It was a ticklish and unwelcome sensation, the price of too much time spent on the marshes, a variant of marsh fever. I had finished with Essex, but it had only just started with me.

BIBLIOGRAPHY

ADAM, DAVID. 8 October 2007. 'Back to nature: £12m plan to let sea flood reclaimed land and recreate lost habitats'. *The Guardian.* https://www.theguardian.com/environment/2007/oct/08/conservation [Accessed 12 June 2018]

ALLINGHAM, MARGERY. 1923 [1974]. *Blackkerchief Dick.* (Kaye and Ward Ltd.)

allingham, Margery. 1941 [1987]. *The Oaken Heart.* (Sarsen Publishing).

ANON. 991 [1981]. *The Battle of Maldon.* (Manchester University Press, ed. D.G. Scragg).

ANON. 5 October 1889. 'The Essex Archipelago'. *The Spectator,* p.14-15

BAKER, J.A. 1967. *The Peregrine.* (Penguin).

BAKER, J.A. 2010. *The Complete Works of J.A. Baker.* Introduction by Cocker, Mark (Harper Collins).

BARING-GOULD, SABINE. 1880 [2002]. *Mehalah: A Story of the Salt Marshes* (Braiswick).

BARING-GOULD, SABINE, 1925. *Further Reminiscences.* John Lane.

BAX, CLIFFORD. 1939. *Highways and Byways in Essex.* (Macmillan and Co.).

BELLOC, HILAIRE. 1925. *The Cruise of the 'Nona'.* (Houghton Mifflin).

BENNETT, ARNOLD. 1914. *From the Log of the Velsa.* (The Century Co.).

BENSUSAN, SAMUEL LEVY. 1938. *Marshland Calling.* (George Routledge and Sons.)

BENSUSAN, SAMUEL LEVY. 1949. *Right Forward Folk.* (Routledge and Keegan Paul.)

BLYTHE, RONALD. 1988. *In Praise of Essex: An Anthology.* (The Alastair Press).

BOOTH, CHARLES. 1886-1903. *Inquiry into the Life and Labour of the People in London.* (LSE, booth.lse.ac.uk).

BRACE, MARIANNE. 6 January 2006. 'Lavinia Greenlaw: Testament of Middle Age'. *The Independent.* https://www.independent.co.uk/arts-entertainment/

books/features/lavinia-greenlaw-testament-of-middle-youth-521740.html [Accessed 12 June 2018]

BRUCE, KEN. 2003. 'The Dengie Hundred Coal Miners', *Essex Harvest*. (Essex Record Office).

CHIN, T. & WELSBY, P. 2004. 'Malaria in the UK: Past, present and future'. *British Medical Journal*, Vol. 80, Issue 949.

CONRAD, JOSEPH. 1902 [1973]. *Heart of Darkness*. (Penguin).

CREME, BENJAMIN. May 2016. 'Return Visit'. *Share International Magazine*. http://share-international.org/magazine/old_issues/2016/2016-05.htm [Accessed 12 June 2018]

DAILY GAZETTE, 'Tiptree Strawberry Race', 30 June 2016

DEFOE, DANIEL. 1724-26 [1972]. *A Tour Through the Whole Island of Great Britain*. (Penguin).

DUCK, ROBERT. 2015. *On the Edge: Coastlines of Britain*. (Edinburgh University Press).

FAUTLEY, MATTHEW AND GARON, JAMES. 2004. *The Essex Coastline – then and now*. (Potton Publishing).

FLEMING, IAN. 1957 [2002]. *From Russia With Love. From Russia With Love, Dr No and Goldfinger*. (Penguin)

GALLICO, PAUL. 1941 (1969). *The Snow Goose*. (Michael Joseph).

GREENLAW, LAVINIA. 2011. 'Essex Kiss'. *The Casual Perfect*. (Faber & Faber).

GRIEVE, HILDA. 1959. *The Great Tide: The story of the 1953 flood disaster in Essex*. (Essex County Council).

HARDY, DENNIS. 2000. *Utopian England: Community Experiments 1900-1945*. (E & FN Spon).

JAMES, M. R. 1904-36 [1987]. *The Penguin Complete Ghost Stories of M.R. James*. (Penguin).

JAMIESON, ALASTAIR. 20 April 2009. 'Historic gates in Frinton-on-Sea removed by Network Rail in dead of night.' *The Daily Telegraph*. https://www.telegraph.

co.uk/news/uknews/5183295/Historic-gates-in-Frinton-on-Sea-removed-by-Network-Rail-in-dead-of-night.html [Accessed 12 June 2018]

JARVIS, STAN. 1989. *Hidden Essex*. (Countryside Books).

JONES, JULIA. 2009. *The Adventures of Margery Allingham*. (Golden Duck).

kingshill, sophia and westwood, Jennifer. 2012. *The Fabled Coast*. (Random House).

LAURANCE, JEREMY. Saturday 20 November 2010. 'Judge Condemns Rehab Clinic Used by the Stars' *The Independent*. https://www.independent.co.uk/life-style/health-and-families/health-news/judge-condemns-rehab-clinic-used-by-the-stars-2139212.html [Accessed 12 June 2018]

LEVERTOV, DENISE. 1966 [2002]. 'A Map of the Western Part of the County of Essex in England'. *Selected Poems* (New Directions).

LONGLEY, MICHAEL. 1969. 'Journey Out of Essex', *No Continuing City*. (Gill and Macmillan).

MACFARLANE, ROBERT. 2007. *The Wild Places*. (Granta).

MACFARLANE, ROBERT. 2012. *The Old Ways*. (Hamish Hamilton).

MASON, CHARLOTTE CRAVEN. 1928. *Essex: Its Forest, Folk and Folklore*. (J.H. Clarke and Co.)

MORPURGO, MICHAEL. 2012 [2016]. *Homecoming*. (Walker Books).

NASH, PAUL. 1949 [2016] *Outline: An Autobiography*. (Lund Humphries).

NORDEN, JOHN. 1594 [1886]. *Speculi Britanniae Pars: An Historical and Chorological Description of the County of Essex*. (The Camden Society).

ORTON, JASON AND WORPOLE, KEN. 2005. *350 Miles: An Essex Journey*. (Essex County Council).

ORTON, JASON AND WORPOLE, KEN. 2013. *The New English Landscape*. (Field Station).

PERRY, SARAH. 2016. *The Essex Serpent*. (Serpent's Tail).

PETER, LAURENCE. 12 April 2018. 'Secrets of the sea bed: Hunt for Stone Age site in North Sea.' *BBC News*. http://www.bbc.co.uk/news/world-europe-43711762 [Accessed 12 June 2018]

POLYBIUS. 1922-27. *The Histories of Polybius*. (Loeb Classical Editions).

PRETTY, JULES. 2011. *This Luminous Coast* (Full Circle Editions).

PRETTY, JULES. 25 September 2012. 'Professor Jules Pretty Explores the Essex Archipelago'. *Essex Life*. http://www.essexlifemag.co.uk/out-about/places/professor-jules-pretty-explores-the-essex-archipelago-1-1571957 [Accessed 12 June 2018]

RABAN, JONATHAN. 1987. *Coasting*. (Picador).

RANSOME, ARTHUR. 1937 [1986]. *We Didn't Mean to Go to Sea*. (Puffin).

RANSOME, ARTHUR. 1939 [1987]. *Secret Water*. (Puffin).

STEPHENS, SIMON. 2006. *Motortown*. (Methuen).

STOKER, BRAM. 1897 [2010]. *Dracula*. (Penguin Classics)

TAYLOR, TERRY. 1961 [2011]. *Baron's Court, All Change*. (New London Editions).

TOMPKINS, HERBERT. W. 1904. *Marsh-Country Rambles*. (Chatto and Windus).

TOWNSEND WARNER, SYLVIA. 1929 [1982]. *The True Heart*. (Virago).

TROLLOPE, ANTHONY. 1876 [1983] *The Prime Minister*. (Oxford World's Classics).

WELLS, H.G. 1898 [1986]. *The War of the Worlds*. (Penguin).

WELLS, H.G. 1916. *Mr Britling Sees it Through*. (The Macmillan Company).

WENTWORTH DAY, JAMES. 1949. *Coastal Adventure*. (George G. Harrap & Co.)

WETHERSPOON, TIM. 2017. 'Tim's Viewpoint, Winter 2017/18'. (Wetherspoons. com) https://www.jdwetherspoon.com/tims-viewpoint/tims-viewpoint [Accessed 12 June 2018]

WILKIN AND SONS LTD. 15 November 2017. 'Modern Slavery Statement'. http://tipcloud.mvad.co.uk/assets/fres/23-modern-slavery-statement.pdf [Accessed 12 June 2018].

WILKIN AND SONS LTD. https://www.tiptree.com/index.php//products/conserves-jams/little-scarlet-strawberry-conserve.html. [Accessed 12 June 2018].

WILLIAMS, CHARLES. 1948. *Judgement at Chelmsford: A Pageant Play*. (Geoffrey Cumberledge).

WYLLIE, CHARLES W. 29 July 1893. 'A Miniature Holland'. *The Graphic*. (reproduced http://www.canveyisland.org/page/a_miniature_holland?path=0p398p401p) [Accessed 12 June 2018]

YEARSLEY, IAN. 2000. *Islands of Essex*. (Ian Henry Publications).